New Vanguard • 4

Churchill Infantry Tank 1941–51

Bryan Perrett • Illustrated by Peter Sarson & Mike Chappell

Published in 1993 by
Osprey Publishing, Elms Court,
Chapel Way, Botley, Oxford OX2 9LP,
United Kingdom.
Email: info@ospreypublishing.com

© 1993 Osprey Publishing Ltd.
Previously published as Vanguard 13
Revised edition
Reprinted 1997, 1999, 2002, 2003, 2004

CIP Data for this publication is available from
the British Library

ISBN 1 85532 297 8

Filmset in Great Britain
Printed in China through World Print Ltd.

FOR A CATALOGUE OF ALL BOOKS PUBLISHED BY
OSPREY MILITARY AND AVIATION PLEASE CONTACT:

The Marketing Manager, Osprey Direct UK, PO Box
140, Wellingborough, Northants,
NN8 2FA, United Kingdom.
Email: info@ospreydirect.co.uk

The Marketing Manager, Osprey Direct USA, c/o MBI
Publishing, PO Box 1, 729 Prospect Avenue, Osceola,
WI 54020, USA.
Email: info@ospreydirectusa.com

www.ospreypublishing.com

Select Bibliography
Barclay, Brigadier C. N., *History of the Duke of
Wellington's Regiment 1919 - 1952*, Wm Clowes

Daniell, D. Scott, *Regimental History The Royal Hampshire
Regiment, Vol III*, Gale & Polden

Nicholson, Colonel W. N., *The Suffolk Regiment 1939 1947*,
East Anglian Magazine Ltd

Perrett, Bryan, *Through Mud and Blood*, Robert Hale

Perrett, Bryan, *The Churchill*, Ian Allen

Privately Printed Histories
The Story of 34 Armoured Brigade

North Irish Horse Battle Report

A Short History of the 51st Battalion Royal Tank Regiment

History of 107 Regiment RAC

Diary of A Squadron, 7th Royal Tank Regiment

*Korean Diary 1950-1951, C Squadron 7th Royal
Tank Regiment*

DEVELOPMENT

For good or for ill, it was the British Army's policy in the years preceding and throughout World War II that infantry operations should have the support of specialist Tank Brigades equipped with purpose-built vehicles. The basic requirement of the Infantry Tank was armour heavy enough to withstand the fire of any anti-tank gun known to be in service during the design phase, and firepower consistent with its task; speed was not considered to be an essential quality, since the pace of any engagement would be geared to that of the infantry.

The first Infantry Tank, the diminutive two man A11, appeared in 1937. The Infantry Tank Mark II A12, better known as the Matilda, began entering service in 1939, and in July of that year an order was also placed for an Infantry Tank Mark III, the Vickers Valentine. It might, perhaps, be wondered why in the circumstances it was

Reflections of an old soldier. There is a hint of nostalgia in the pose of Winston Churchill, veteran of the North-West Frontier and the cavalry charge at Omdurman, as he watches some of the first tanks to bear his name drive past during an exercise. (This, and all other photographs not specifically credited otherwise, are from the Imperial War Museum collections.)

considered necessary to embark in September 1939 upon yet a fourth design, to be known as the A20.

Predicting requirements for a future war is never easy. Many senior officers felt that the fighting along the Western Front would take the form of the later 1918 battles, with the enemy occupying heavily defended zones, and requested the Superintendent of Tank Design to produce pilot models of a Heavy Infantry Tank with a wide trench crossing capacity and the ability to drive over the worst shell-torn ground.

Not surprisingly, the design incorporated a high top run for the tracks, so that the vehicle's hull contained a hint of its World War I ancestors; this

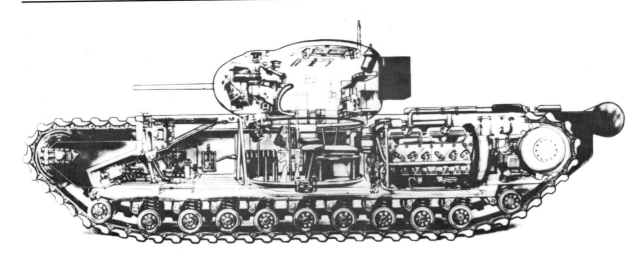

Cutaway view of the Churchill Mark I showing Internal layout of driving, *fighting, engine and transmission compartments. (RAC Tank Museum)*

was further accentuated by the main armament, consisting of two 2pdrs., being housed in sponsons slung on either side. However, by the time Harland and Wolff Limited produced the first prototypes in June 1940, it had been decided that the exterior sponson idea did not work, (2pdr. now being located in a top turret with all round traverse, and the second in the hull alongside the driver).

The A20 appeared at the height of the Dunkirk crisis, at a time when the British Army found itself desperately short of every type of fighting vehicle. To accelerate production the A20 was scaled down by Dr H. E. Merritt, Director of Tank Design, in conjunction with a team of engineers from Vauxhall Motors Limited, whose Twin-Six engine was to have powered the A20. The resulting design, known offficially as the A22, was named 'Churchill' in the interests of national morale, and Vauxhall were instructed to have it in production within one year – an incredibly short period, which virtually eliminated any possibility of detailed user and development trials. Working straight from the drawing board, Vauxhall succeeded in hitting their target, and from June 1941 vehicles began to arrive at their regiments. With them came the User Handbook, containing the manufacturer's honest admission that they were far from satisfied with the automotive aspects of their product:

'All those things which we know are not as they should be will be put right. In nearly every case the cure has already been found, and it will be introduced as soon as the new material or new parts become available.

'Please do not draw the wrong conclusions from this frank statement of defects. The Mark IV Infantry Tank is a good vehicle. The troubles which have emerged from recent tests of the pilot model are not in any way abnormal. The only abnormal factor is that, having found them, we are not in a position to put them right before production begins.

'Times, however, are not normal. Fighting vehicles are urgently required, and instructions have been received to proceed with the vehicle as it is rather than hold up production.'

Some of the defects known to exist at the time the handbook went to press are listed below:

Seizure of bogies, remedied by replacing phosphor bronze fulcrum shafts and bearings with chromium plate and white metal respectively.

Bolts worked loose on the connection between the sprocket and final drive, in the muff coupling between the gearbox and final drive, and in the main brake drums, and were replaced by higher-tensility parts with shake-proof washers.

Track-link failures, remedied by improved casting and design. Blown gaskets and leaking oil seals, corrected by redesign and use of more suitable materials.

Pre-vaporisation of fuel caused by the location of petrol pumps and fuel lines above the engine, eliminated by locating those parts in cooler areas.

Corrosion of flexible pipes in the lubrication system, causing extensive oil leaks after short periods of running, remedied by the use of alternative materials for the pipes.

Rapid clutch wear, eliminated by tougher linings.

Lack of waterproofing on the ignition harness, corrected by modification.

Further defects were reported by Vauxhall's own engineering teams, seconded to regiments which were attempting to carry out training programmes; and occasionally units produced their own expedient solution to a problem, as in the case of 147 (Hampshire) Regiment RAC: 'Our main trouble lay in the transmission link between the driver and the gearbox. There was a rod in the gearbox which actuated the gears and this rod was constantly breaking. Replacements were almost impossible to obtain and it wasn't until we moved to Norfolk to join a brigade that we solved this problem. The Technical Adjutant visited all the small garages and workshops in the county

Mark Is of 48 RTR coming ashore during an amphibious exercise. The white bar under the regiment's tactical number '175' signifies troops under Army command. The air louvres have been removed because of space limitations aboard the LCTs.

and bought up every Ford half-axle he could find, having discovered that this axle was stronger and took the place exactly of the defective rod.'

The cause and official cure for the problem is described by Mr H. E. Ashfield, who was Dr Merritt's chief gearbox designer at the time: 'The original selector forks which shifted the gears were designed in nickel bronze. Unfortunately, nickel being in short supply, deliveries were made in aluminium bronze which was a much weaker material in that it flexes more easily. Consequently gears did not engage fully and in some instances jumped out of mesh under load. The vibration and chatter resulting from this caused failures of both the selector fork and the selector rod to which the fork was attached. The cure was to increase the proportions of the fork to allow for the weaker material, and to increase the diameter of the rod. This proved very effective and to my recollection there was no repetition of the problem.'

On the early production models the air-intake louvres pointed downwards, but during training it was soon discovered that the powerful fan drew in quantities of leaves and dust, effectively starving the engine of air, and on all subsequent models the louvers pointed upwards.

These constant modifications and improvements succeeded in producing a vehicle which was mechanically reliable by the time the Churchill was committed to action in 1942.

In layout the Churchill followed conventional lines, and was divided into four compartments. The driving compartment housed the driver and hull gunner, behind which was the fighting compartment, surmounted by the turret, the crew of which consisted of the vehicle commander, gunner and loader-operator. The engine compartment contained the engine, radiators and petrol tanks, and the rear compartment housed the gearbox, steering and main brakes, air compressor and the auxiliary and power traverse generators. The tank was powered by a 12-cylinder Vauxhall Bedford Twin-Six 350hp engine, which could produce a road speed of 15½ mph, this dropping to 8mph across country. The suspension consisted of 22 independently sprung small-diameter bogies which

A variation on the Mark I theme, in which a Besa machine gun has replaced the 3in. howitzer in the hull. On Marks I and II the co-axial Besa was located to the right of the main armament. The vehicle carries an auxiliary fuel tank. (RAC Tank Museum)

could be removed and replaced as separate units. Maximum armour thickness was 102mm, increased to 152mm on the later Marks.

The hull was unusual for a British vehicle in that sponson escape hatches were provided for the crew, these being a legacy of the original A20 concept. The Churchill was also unusual in that it was steered by a tiller-bar, while the four-speed Merritt-Brown gearbox provided controlled differential steering, thus permitting the vehicle to neutral-turn about its own axis.

In general, the Churchill's subsequent development history follows that of British tank armament. By 1940 the 2pdr. was considered to be obsolete but was still being produced in quantity to replace losses in France, as time could not be spared for factories to re-tool for the replacement 6pdr. The **Churchill Mark I**, therefore, carried a 2pdr. gun and a co-axial 7.92mm Besa machine gun in a cast turret, with a 3in. howitzer mounted in the hull. This arrangement gave the tank a balanced armour piercing/high explosive capability, as the 2pdr. did not at that time fire an HE round. The Mark I saw service at Dieppe and in Tunisia, and a few soldiered on as late as the 1944 Gothic Line battles in Italy. An alternative arrangement in which the 3in howitzer was replaced by a second Besa has been described in some sources as the Mark II.

The **Mark II** proper saw the transposition of the 2pdr. and the 3in. howitzer to produce a better close support tank, but was produced in small numbers only.

The **Mark III** carried a 6pdr. main armament in a distinctive welded turret. This version saw the standardization of the Churchill's secondary armament to one co-axial and one hull Besa, and also the installation of track catwalks, which had been absent on the earlier Marks.

The **Mark IV** saw a reversion to the cast turret, the vehicle's main armament being the 6pdr. Early models carrying the Mark V version of the gun can be identified by the counter-weight on the muzzle.

The **Mark V** was a close support tank equipped with a 95mm howitzer which carried a prominent counter-weight on the muzzle. The vehicle provided squadrons with an extra punch when engaging bunkers, strongpoints and buildings. Only 10 per cent of the total Churchill production was given over to this support-tank role.

The **Mark VI** was the first Churchill to be equipped with the British 75mm gun with muzzle brake, but was otherwise very similar to the Mark IV, a number of which were up-gunned to Mark VI standards.

The **Mark VII** also mounted the 75mm gun, but was radically different from the earlier Marks in that maximum armour thickness was increased from 102mm to 152mm. This, and a slightly wider hull, had the effect of raising the tank's weight to 40 tons, with a consequent reduction in road speed to 12½ mph. With this Mark the previously square sponson escape doors were replaced by round hatches. The Mark VII turret had been completely redesigned and was a composite of cast and welded parts, a low cupola and blade-vane sight being provided for the commander. The recessed rectangular mantlets fitted to Marks III-VI had been vulnerable to bullet splash caused by lateral fire, and although this arrangement was maintained on the Mark VII, additional protection was later provided by external shoulder castings on either side of the mantlet. The **Mark VIII** was simply a close support version of the Mark VII, equipped with the same 95mm howitzer carried by the Mark V.

In addition to these basic Marks there was an extensive refitting programme designed to utilize the older vehicles to the full. Thus a Mark III or IV hull fitted with appliqué armour plating to bring it up to Mark VII standard became known as the **Mark IX**; a similarly up-armoured Mark VI hull with a Mark VII turret became the **Mark X**; and a reinforced Mark V with the Mark VIII turret became the **Mark XI**. There were also minor variations on the theme in which up-gunned tanks retained their old turrets, and sometimes a cupola was added retrospectively.

Two Mark IIIs of 'A' Squadron, North Irish Horse photographed near Hunt's Gap during Operation 'Ochsenkopf'.

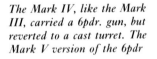

The Mark IV, like the Mark III, carried a 6pdr. gun, but reverted to a cast turret. The Mark V version of the 6pdr often carried a counterweight on the muzzle.

The Mark VI, seen here in Normandy, was the first Churchill to mount the British 75mm gun. The 6th Guards Tank Brigade sign can just be seen left of the hull Besa.

The **Churchill NA 75** was simply a Mark IV equipped with the Sherman 75mm gun and mantlet, and represents one of the most ingenious conversions in AFV history. It was the brainchild of Captain Percy Morrell, REME, who at the end of 1943 was Second-in-Command of 665 Tank Troops Workshops at Le Khroub, Algeria.

Morrell had observed that in the bright North African sunlight the Churchill's recessed mantlet cast a deep shadow which provided the German gunners with an aiming point, and in fact 60 per cent of Churchill casualties in the Medjerda Valley had been caused by hits on or around the mantlet. He was also aware that the Churchill crews were hampered by lack of a 6pdr. high explosive round during their engagements with anti-tank guns, whereas Sherman crews had no such difficulty. (This omission had been rectified by the time the Tank Brigades reached Italy). Numbers of Shermans had been collected for scrapping, although in many cases the 75mm main armament was almost new; and he felt that by removing these guns, complete with mantlet, and installing them in Churchill IVs, the two problems would be solved simultaneously.

His calculations proved that it could be done, and at length he was given permission to try by Major-General W. S. Tope, Director of Mechanical Engineering in the Central Mediterranean Theatre.

While the front of the Sherman turret was flat, that of the Churchill IV was rounded, so it was necessary to rebate cheeks until a satisfactory seat was obtained for the Sherman mantlet, which was then welded into place. However, as Morrell noted, 'In the Sherman the front face of the turret and consequently the gun mounting was laid back from the vertical some 30 degrees. The gun barrel protruded through the mantlet and moved in a slot. The effect of welding the mantlet to the front face of the Churchill turret was to limit the elevation to a little over the horizontal and to permit depression to a much greater degree than was required. To compensate for this came the simple expedient of elongating the top of the slot by some eight inches and welding the piece cut out back into the bottom of the slot.'

The major difficulty arose in reconciling the two different crew practices. In the American vehicle the loader was on the left of the gun and

the gunner on the right; in the British vehicle these positions were reversed, so that as things stood the 75mm breech opened inconveniently to the left, i.e. towards the gunner. After some careful thought Morrell discovered a way of turning the gun 180 degrees within its mounting so that the breech opened to the right, and installed cross-over linkages for the gun controls.

Range trials showed that the Churchill provided a steadier firing platform for the 75mm than did the Sherman, and an increase in range was recorded. Orders were immediately given for large-scale conversion to begin, under Morrell's direction, at 16 Base Workshops near Bone. Top priority was accorded to the project, which was codenamed 'Whitehot', and in the three months to June 1944 some 200 were converted.

The Churchill NA 75s (North Africa 75mm) served in Italy, notably at the Gothic Line, and were favourably reported on by their crews. It is pleasant to record that Percy Morrell's initiative and ingenuity earned his promotion to Major and the award of the M.B.E.; he had been warned at the outset that if he failed, and so rendered an expensive Churchill unserviceable, his military career would receive no further advancement.

However, in spite of the sustained increase in the power of its main armament, the Churchill

The Crocodile flame-thrower was a conversion of the basic Churchill Mark VII; the latter was easily identified by its composite cast/ welded turret, circular escape doors and mantlet shoulders. (RAC Tank Museum)

remained under-gunned throughout its career and was consistently outranged when opposed by German tanks and self-propelled guns. In an effort to achieve parity, work was begun in the autumn of 1943 on a Super Churchill which would mount the 17pdr. gun. Six prototypes appeared in May 1945 under the title of A43 Black Prince, but by then the less complicated Centurion Mark I, which also carried the 17pdr. and offered identical armour protection, was beginning its production run, and it was decided not to proceed with further development along these lines.

Thus, in addition to mounting a wider variety of armament than any other tank, the Churchill's basic adaptability made it one of the most important British designs of the war. Altogether 5,640 Churchills were built under Vauxhall parentage by heavy engineering concerns in the United Kingdom, and served in such diverse theatres as the Western Desert, Tunisia, North-West Europe, Italy, Burma and Korea. Some even saw action in Russia; as part of the Soviet assistance programme a number of Marks I–III were despatched to the USSR in August 1942. At this period the Red Army held a

decisive lead in the field of tank armament and had little use for the 2pdr. and 6pdr. guns, which were usually stripped out and replaced by their own 76.2mm models.

OPERATIONAL HISTORY

It has often been said that war is a compound of long periods of boredom and short periods of intense fear. From 1943 onwards, the armoured divisions tended to be detailed for specific operations of comparatively short duration, but the tank brigades, although occasionally out of the line for months at a time, remained in continuous action for much longer periods. Alan Gilmour, a tank driver of 48 RTR, summed up the common experience when he wrote of the Gothic Line: 'In the weeks which followed, as the assault grew in fury, hideous nights pressed on days of horror. We lost men, we lost tanks, almost we lost hope of survival.'

After a day spent in a series of minor tactical situations designed to overcome some aspect of the enemy's defence, and generally carried out under the muzzles of German tanks and anti-tank guns, the Churchills would be withdrawn after dusk and go into leaguer. Here maintenance and replenishment would continue for several hours, during which the crews would attempt to cook themselves a hot meal. The short period left for sleep would invariably be interrupted by guard duty, and long before first light the tanks would be moving through the darkness again to marry up with the infantry with whom they would fight the next day's battles. It was a numbing process which by its very continuity ground away at men's physical and mental reserves and which bore down heavily on squadron and troop commanders, who not only forfeited food and sleep attending

orders groups and carrying out route reconnaissance, but also spent much of their time in action on their feet alongside their infantry opposite numbers.

Notwithstanding, morale in the tank brigades remained high and they earned the unstinting praise of the infantry formations with whom they fought. They were admired by the armoured divisions, but not envied: 'It was a job we should have hated,' was the comment of a former commander of 7th Armoured Division, himself a veteran of Beda Fomm, Sidi Rezegh and Imphal.

On the virtues and vices of the Churchill itself the crews were unanimous. They welcomed the stout armour and the sponson escape hatches, the tank's ability to climb the steepest hills and wallow through the deepest mud, and the additional internal stowage space permitted by the wide hull, but they regretted the absence of a main armament which would put them on equal terms with the German tank crews. The maintenance work-load, too, was a heavy one, requiring, inter alia, the greasing of 22 bogies, usually in darkness, after coming out of action. There were also a number of minor disadvantages which had to be lived with, such as the curtailment of the driver's lateral vision by the long forward track horns; the noise level inside the vehicle caused by the high track run; the dense fug built up when the guns were in action, which the extractor fan seemed incapable of clearing; the effect of the sirocco fan on dry ground, sending a blast of dust under the tank's belly to be sucked into the vehicle through the driver's and turret hatches; the lack of internal drainage channels in the early Marks, which could

The Mark VIII was very similar to the Mark V, which also mounted the 95mm howitzer, but can *be recognized by the circular escape hatches and the Mark VII turret. (RAC Tank Museum)*

result in water slopping round the interior after a downpour; and an unnerving tendency to run away without warning if the hydraulic brake lines failed when the vehicle was out of gear, the results never being less than dramatic. In spite of such idiosyncrasies the crews remained fond of their mount, and were quick to point out that the Churchill could operate on going the Sherman could not, and was less prone than the American vehicle to catch fire if penetrated.

ORGANIZATION AND TACTICS

The tank brigades consisted of three Infantry Tank regiments, a brigade workshops and supply services. Each regiment contained an RHQ Troop of four Churchills, a Recce Troop of twelve Stuarts, a Light Aid Detachment (REME), 'A' and 'B' transport echelons, and three tank squadrons. During the Normandy fighting RHQ also included a troop of Crusader AA tanks for local air defence. As the Allied air superiority was all but total, these vehicles were employed in the ground support role, with devastating results. This troop was later removed as being surplus to requirements.

Churchills of 6th Guards Tank Brigade in Cleve during the Reichswald battle. The nearest vehicle is a Mark VI fitted with additional hull armour to bring it up to Mark VII standard, the result being known as the Mark IX.

The internal organization of the squadrons include an SHQ Troop of four Churchills, at least one c which would be a close support tank; four three tank Churchill troops, an ARV and, during th later stages of the war, a bridgelayer. A number c Daimler scout cars were also held by regimenta and squadron headquarters for liaison wit infantry units.

When originally formed the tank brigades carrie the prefix Army, although this was droppe with the establishment of the so-called 'mixed divisions in mid-1942, each such division containin one tank and two infantry brigades. In practic this did not work as the division lacked th reserve which would normally have been provide by the third infantry brigade, and the idea wa abandoned early in 1943 the tank brigades revertin to Army control.

The policy of Army commanders was t concentrate the tank brigades' strength in area where the infantry divisions were fighting t effect a breach in the enemy's defences, through which the armoured divisions could be passe to exploit into the open country beyond. Th

Medjerda Valley, the Hitler and Gothic Lines, the Normandy Beachhead and the Reichswald all offer good examples of concentrated Infantry Tank employment, although an exploitation did not result in every case.

It was normal practice for a tank brigade to support an infantry division. Thus, a regiment would support an infantry brigade, a squadron a battalion and a troop a company, but the rule was by no means inflexible. The tanks would remain under infantry control for the duration of the operation, but would fight together as conventional squadrons if the enemy armour attempted to intervene.

The tank brigades did not, therefore, fight as tactical formations, although a rare exception to this can be found in 6th Guards Tank Brigade's action at Caumont. It was almost as rare for a Churchill regiment to fight together, although its squadrons might find themselves supporting adjacent infantry battalions. There were occasions, however, when an attack was going badly and the tanks' commanding officer came forward to co-ordinate his squadrons to the infantry's best advantage, as did Lieutenant-Colonel Timmis of 51 RTR at Bou Arada.

The basic tactical team consisted of an infantry battalion supported by a Churchill squadron with an artillery battery on immediate call through the Forward Observation Officer's radio link. The FOO, an artillery officer, accompanied the tanks in his own vehicle, which was usually a Stuart in Tunisia and Italy, although in Northwest Europe he was allocated a Churchill. His function was to neutralize an area which was holding up the advance, and to institute defensive fire tasks if the enemy counter-attacked. If he became a casualty his duties would be taken over temporarily by one of the tank officers, generally the squadron's second-in-command or 'battle captain', all of whom were trained in the task.

Infantry/tank tactics in the early war years required the tanks to arrive on the objective in two waves just ahead of the infantry, with whom they would remain until the captured ground had been consolidated and the battalion's own anti-tank guns brought forward and emplaced. At Alamein the practice had been radically different, the infantry making their attacks by night and the 'I' tanks moving up to join them by first light so as to beat off the inevitable counter-attack until the anti-tank guns arrived. Both methods were employed by the Churchill tank brigades in Tunisia, but during the subsequent fighting in Italy, France and the Low Countries a totally different technique had to be evolved.

This came about partly because of advances in weapon technology, and partly because of the changing nature of the battlefield. The development of the *Panzerfaust*, the German equivalent of the bazooka, meant that tank-hunting teams could conceal themselves in close country and wait until the tanks were almost on top of them before opening fire, often with fatal results, since the hollow-charge bomb could penetrate any armour in service. To counter this, the infantry led the attack through standing crops, orchards, woods and vineyards, flushing out the *Panzerfaust* teams as they went.

In more open country the tanks led, but were immediately vulnerable to the fire of the emplaced Tigers, assault guns and *Panzerjäger* upon which the German concept of defence now rested. The solution to this problem was the attachment of one or two troops of tank destroyers to each Churchill squadron. The tank destroyers, 3in. M10s or 17pdr. Achilles and Archers, carefully selected their fire position before the attack started,

The Churchill NA 75, including the signatures of those concerned with the subsequent conversion programme. (Major Percy Morrell, M.B.E.)

The interior of the NA 75 turret, showing the 75mm gun turned to the right, and the crossover linkage. The NA 75's co-axial armament was a Browning, the butt of which grounded on the power traverse mechanism, as shown on the left. The mounting was modified so that the gun followed the main armament up to the point of grounding and then remained static while the latter continued in elevation. (Major Percy Morrell, M.B.E.)

equipped with Shermans. Being less we armoured but having better gun control equipmen than the Churchills, these vehicles formed the secon echelon of the assault and often provided direct c semi-indirect gunfire support from layback position Following the disbandment of a brigade during th winter months more Churchills became availabl and regiments fought the 1945 battles with complete establishment.

The infantry/tank operations of 1944–45 wer therefore, governed by a highly professional inter dependence between arms. The tanks would de with the enemy's infantry, machine gun post: bunkers and minor fortifications, engage hi armour, and stand by in the counter-attack rôl until a captured position was secure; the infantr would protect the tanks from *Panzerfaust* team: stalk anti-tank guns, sieze and hold the objectiv the tank destroyers would prevent their Germa counterparts from engaging the out-gunne Churchills during the combined advance; an the artillery, through the FOO, could put dow concentrations exactly when and where they wer needed, in addition to firing the preparatory barrag For specific operations an assault engineer elemen

and engaged the enemy armour throughout its duration. Sometimes the tank destroyers would take the place of the Churchills during the consolidation phase, while the latter retired to a forward rally point to replenish and the battalion anti-tank guns were dug in.

In Italy the position was slightly complicated by a shortage of Churchills during 1944, which meant that two troops in each 'I' tank squadron were

The l7pdr. 'Super Churchill', Black Prince, was abandoned in favour of the less complicated   *Centurion Mark I, which carried the same armour and armament. (RAC Tank Museum)*

might also be included in the order of battle, the various types of AVRE, Crab and Ark being supplied by 79th Armoured Division on the Western Front and by 25 Armoured Engineer Brigade in Italy. (See Variants section)

No account of the Churchills' tactical employment would be complete without mention of the morale effect of such support on the infantry with whom the tanks worked. In addition to the obvious point of casualties inflicted on the enemy and lives saved by their presence, the tanks assisted in a variety of less apparent ways, carrying dannert wire, small arms ammunition and other consolidation stores during the attack itself, and providing the reliable communications link which the infantry lacked. After the action the lightly wounded could be treated from the tanks' first aid kits, while the more serious cases were carried to safety on the engine decks. These diverse services, and a wealth of shared experience, established such mutual confidence that implementation of the combined battle drill became instinctive.

OPERATION 'JUBILEE'

During August 1942, 147 (Hampshire) Regiment RAC was stationed at Worthing on the south coast of England. It was regimental practice to maintain a listening watch on its No. 19 wireless sets, a boring duty which, throughout the early hours of 19 August promised little diversion. However, towards dawn, freak reception brought a spate of transmissions. The accents were Canadian, but the speakers were obviously tank crew, and the operators began to log each message. It was not easy, since the rapid speech was that of men under stress, overlaid with the sound of gunfire. The transmissions continued for several hours, but petered out by mid-morning.

It was not until the newspapers began printing reports of the raid on Dieppe that the signals logs started to make sense. They told at first hand the tragic story of 2nd Canadian Division's decimation on the beaches in front of the town, as seen from

The AVRE (Assault Vehicle Royal Engineers) was capable of performing a wide variety of assault engineering tasks. As the photograph shows, its 290mm mortar could be used with devastating effect against concrete.

The Churchill Bridgelayer, with bridge raised from its cradles to show launching mechanism. (RAC Tank Museum)

the Churchill turrets of 14th Army Tank Battalion, otherwise known as the Calgary Regiment.

The object of the Dieppe raid was to test the defences on a sector of enemy-held coast known to be heavily fortified, and to apply the lessons learned when the Allies returned to continental Europe at a later date. As far as the Calgary Regiment was concerned its tasks were to support the Essex Scottish Regiment and Royal Hamilton Light Infantry off the beach and into the town, following which the tanks would shoot up the airfield at St Aubyn and attack the chateau of Arques-les-Batailles, which was suspected of being a divisional headquarters.

The beach, flanked by the East and West Headlands, consisted of heavily banked and graded shingle, and was backed by a sea wall which for most of its length was too high for the Churchills to scale. Beyond lay a wide stretch of open ground that had once been ornamental gardens, the Boulevard Foch, and then a row of hotels and houses. The whole area was covered from several directions by carefully sited anti-tank and machine gun posts, and the exits from the boulevard into the town had been sealed by concrete barriers.

The Calgarys' Churchills had been waterproofed and equipped with deep-wading exhausts which would see them ashore from the LCTs. To counter the effect of the shingle, which would scatter and slide about under the tracks, the first tanks out of the landing craft would carry an elementary bobbin which would unroll a carpet of hessian and wooden paling strips ahead of the vehicles and up to the sea wall, along which the others would follow. Where the sea wall was too high to cross, engineer teams would blow down sections to form ramps, and then go on to demolish the anti-tank walls blocking the routes into the town; however the engineers were on foot, and terribly vulnerable.

It goes almost without saying that the overall planning of the operation demanded that the East and West Headlands should be secured before the assault on the town beach went in; but because of a combination of the most evil bad luck and a certain amount of bad management, neither headland had been taken when the Essex, Hamilton and Calgary landing craft grounded on the shingle to find themselves trapped in a natural killing ground. Cross-fire from the headlands flayed the beach, while the landing craft were raked from the buildings beyond the sea wall. Some platoons were shot down as they crossed the lowered ramps, while the survivors of others tried to scrape what cover they could for themselves among the loose stones.

It had been decided that the tanks would land in four waves, made up as follows:

First Wave; two groups totalling nine tanks, with the infantry.

Second Wave; one group of twelve tanks.

Third Wave; one group of sixteen tanks.

Fourth Wave; remainder of regiment.

The first wave included three 'Oke' flamethrowers (see Variants section), one of which left its LCT too early and drowned, while the second had its track shot away and the third erupted into an inferno when the flame gun fuel tank was penetrated. Three more tanks lost tracks or bellied in the shingle; but the three survivors, *Cougar*, *Cheetah* and *Cat*, successfully crossed the beach on their carpet and climbed the sea wall, to be joined by four tanks from the second wave, whose fate had been as mixed as that of the first.

The third wave was committed at the same time as the reserve infantry battalion, the Fusiliers Mont Royal, but only ten tanks reached the shore due to damage sustained by the LCTs as the covering smoke screen began to disperse. Of these seven left the beach, while one remained jammed across the wall, engaging the houses with its gun fully depressed. The Calgarys' commanding officer, Lt.-Col. Andrews, was shot down in the shallows after extricating his crew from their tank, which had been launched prematurely into deep water.

Approximately half the tanks ashore had now crossed the wall and were engaging the defences beyond. A French tank serving as a pillbox was blown apart by *Cougar*, while *Cheetah* engaged bunkers in the gardens, cutting down the occupants when they tried to make a run for it. Other tanks succeeded in suppressing the fire coming from the houses and hotels, one building being rammed to bring it down around the defenders' ears; but the Churchills could not break into the town because of the concrete road-blocks, since the demolition teams had either been killed or were pinned down by the murderous cross-fire on the beach.

The Calgarys' fourth wave did not land, for by 0900hrs it was clear to the operational commander that further effort was useless, and he gave the order to withdraw. All but six of the tanks returned to the beach, where an unsuccessful rescue was attempted; but of all the crews ashore, only one man succeeded in reaching England. The regiment's casualties amounted to 13 killed, 4 wounded and 157 taken prisoner. That evening, with a consideration rare in total war, the Luftwaffe dropped a bundle of photographs onto the Calgarys' barracks in Seaford, showing those who had survived the raid

10 tank destroyers ossing a causeway of hurchill 'Arks' during the othic Line fighting. From 44 Churchill squadrons ught with tank destroyer pport. The leading vehicle carries the markings of a British V Corps self-propelled anti-tank regiment, and almost certainly belongs to one of the batteries of 105 Anti-Tank Regiment, RA.

e Churchill ARV Mark complete with dummy gun and turret. (RAC Tank Museum)

For the Canadian infantry Operation 'Jubilee' d been a bloodbath; but the terrible price they iid led directly to the development of the moured engineer vehicles with which the Allied mies led their assault landings on 6 June 1944, th comparatively small loss of life for such an ormous undertaking.

AFRICA

here was a feeling in the United Kingdom that e Churchill's cooling system was quite inadequate r desert warfare, and to prove or disprove this gument six Mark IIIs were shipped to Egypt in ne to take part in the Second Battle of Alamein,

manned by a small scratch unit known as 'Kingforce' and commanded by Maj. Norris King of the Royal Gloucester Hussars.

It was originally intended that the unit would support 7th Motor Brigade, but due to congestion in the minefield gaps during the first days of the battle, it actually fought under the direct command of 1st Armoured Division.

'Kingforce' went into action twice, the first engagement taking place near Kidney Ridge on 27 October 1942, the second being the major tank battle of Tel el Aqqaqir on 3 November. In these two actions the six vehicles absorbed 106 hits from AP and HE projectiles, resulting in one tank burned out, one immobilized with track damage, and one with a jammed turret, seven men being killed and eight wounded. The burned-out tank was penetrated by one 75mm and two 50mm rounds of obviously enemy origin, and one of these reached the petrol tank. There were also three 6pdr. penetrations in the turret rear, and one in the transmission compartment, probably the result of Australian anti-tank gunners firing into the vehicle to speed its burning and clear their line of sight from drifting smoke. (In return 'Kingforce' claimed five enemy tanks and three anti-tank guns).

The technical report was written by Lt. A. L. Deans, RTR, who had been closely involved with Churchill development since the days of the A20, and began: 'These tanks were used on both occasions a considerable distance in advance of the Sherman tanks which formed the main attack. They came under very heavy fire and stood up remarkably well... The tank crews were composed of men newly sent out from training regiments in England who had a slight acquaintance with the Churchill tank, but no experience of desert warfare. The tank NCOs had some experience of the desert, but had never seen a Churchill before. The unit went into action thirteen days after being formed, by which time the crews were beginning to know the maintenance routine... Some tanks did occasionally have trouble in starting when hot, but this was usually due to the inexperience of the driver.' The report also pointed out that no overheating had occurred, but emphasized that the

'Crabbing', i.e. sliding sideways when moving across a steep hillside, is a danger feared by most tank crews. Unless stopped immediately, the slide can become a runaway or worse–as in the case of this Churchill Mark I: a series of rolls in which the turret is shed with fatal results.

tanks had operated on the northern sector during the cooler months of October and November, and that use further south during the summer might produce different results. An important and immediate consequence of the report was the decision to despatch two Churchill tank brigades to support 1st Army in Tunisia.

'Kingforce' was disbanded immediately after the battle, but a last reference to the only Churchills to fight in the Western Desert appears in a situation report of 5 November prepared by Col. P. W. H. Whiteley, principal Army Recovery Officer, for the benefit of the DDME 8th Army:

'Five Churchills at present at junction of Moon Track and Springbok Road are under temporary command 86 Sub Area pending evacuation to Delta. One of these has a damaged sprocket which is being changed locally with that of the u/s Churchill [i.e. the total loss]. These are low priority for evacuation and will be dealt with via Hammam railhead.'

The first Churchill formation to serve in North Africa was 25 Tank Brigade (North Irish Horse, 51 RTR and 142 (Suffolk) Regiment RAC), which arrived at the height of Rommel's drive against the American IInd Corps in the Kasserine Pass area. The Germans' strategic objective was to wheel north after penetrating the American front, and so compel the withdrawal of all Allied forces in northern Tunisia, which would find themselves in danger of being cut off. In this design the ro[ad] junction at Le Kef was of vital importance an[d] with other troops, 142 Regiment was rushed sou[th] to counter the threat, some tanks being carried [by] transporter, others covering 100 miles on the[ir] own tracks in twenty-four hours. It was anticipat[ed] that the enemy would approach Le Kef along t[he] Sbeitla-Sbiba road, and a defensive front w[as] established south of Sbiba. On 21 February t[wo] troops and a Cold-stream Guards plato[on] launched a counter-attack which captured a rid[ge] east of the road, eliminating several machine g[uns] and anti-tank positions, but an advance to a furth[er] ridge was checked with the loss of three tan[ks]. That night the enemy disengaged and withdrew [to] the south. Even as the last echoes of the Kasseri[ne] Pass operations were dying away, the Axis mount[ed] a fresh offensive code-named *'Ochsenkopf'* (Bul[l's] head), against the northern and central sectors [of] the front, in the belief that most of the Allied reser[ves] had been drawn away to the south. The southe[rn] horn of this 'Bull's Head' was directed at El Arous[sa] from which roads ran north to Medjez el Bab a[nd] east to Bou Arada. The area was held by a scrat[ch] force called 'Y' Division, with 'A' Squadron 51 RT[R] and 'C' Squadron 142 Regiment under comman[d].

On 26 February the Suffolk squadron fough[t a] brilliant solo action some miles to the east [of] the town, their opponents being two battalions [of] the *'Hermann Göring'* Parachute Division and [a] supporting Panzer company. Firing from hull-do[wn] positions, the Churchills knocked out four ene[my] tanks, disabled three more and destroyed [an] 88mm anti-tank gun for the loss of one vehic[le]. Bereft of their armour, the Germany infant[ry] declined to advance.

The paratroopers modified their plan of atta[ck] and began to outflank El Aroussa from the nor[th]. During the evening of 27 February 'Y' Divisio[n's] commander was informed that the Medjez el B[ab] road had been cut, and he decided to send ou[t a] reconnaissance in force the following morning [to] test the enemy's strength. The troops detail[ed] included 'A' Squadron 51 RTR under Maj. E. [T.] Hadfield, a Coldstream Guards company and [a] troop of 25pdrs. The reconnaissance proceed[ed] slowly and methodically until by 1600hrs it w[as] earing some buildings known as Steamroller Farm, beyond which the road climbed to the summit of a pass.

The tanks were suddenly engaged by a complex of anti-tank guns dug in around the farm, and immediately returned the fire while the Guardsmen deployed. At the height of the fire-fight a squadron of Stukas howled down to add to the pandemonium, their bombs bursting on and around the tanks, which were prevented from closing in on the farm by a series of deep wadis. Although several anti-tank guns were knocked out, the Churchills suffered severely from the fire of the remainder as well as the bombings. Hadfield advised Divisional HQ of the position but was told that he must force his way past the farm and into the high ground beyond at all costs.

The squadron leader detailed his No. 1 Troop, commanded by Capt. E. D. Hollands, to carry out the order. By now the troop had been reduced to a single vehicle, *Adventurer*, which seemed to bear a charmed life as it roared along the causeway on which the road passed the farm. Rounding a bend, Hollands came face to face with an '88', but got in the first shot, wrecking the gun. *Adventurer* began to climb, still on the road, and turned another blind corner to find a second '88' only thirty yards distant. The big gun fired, grazed the turret, fired again, and missed completely; its crew took to their heels, to be cut down by the hull gunner.

n hard, dusty ground the
Churchill's 'Sirocco' fan
would send a blast of dust

under the stationary
vehicle's belly and then draw
it in through the hatches.

Hollands now swung off the road and headed for the summit over steep and rocky going, engaging various positions on the way. He was joined minutes later by a second tank commanded by Lt. J. G. Renton, and the two crews had what the regimental history describes as 'the shoot of their lives', destroying the Germans' entire transport echelon, which was harboured beyond the crest, and two PzKpfw IIIs which unwisely tried to intervene. When the order to retire came, Hollands found himself stalled with flat batteries almost a mile inside the enemy position. *Adventurer* was tow-started by Renton's vehicle, both crews working under fire to attach the heavy wire hawser, and the tanks rejoined the squadron.

Hadfield disengaged and retired slowly, leaving the enemy to lick their wounds. 'A' squadron had lost a number of vehicles, which were recovered when the Germans evacuated the farm a few days later, and every tank had sustained some form of damage. In return, however, it had destroyed two tanks, eight anti-tank guns, two light anti-aircraft guns, two mortars and 25 assorted vehicles, and had inflicted up to 200 personnel casualties.

Wireless intercept operators were delighted by an hysterical transmission from the German commander at Steamroller Farm to the *Fliegerführer II Afrika*, to the effect that he had been attacked by 'a mad tank battalion which had scaled impossible heights' and compelled his ultimate withdrawal[1].

The northern horn of the 'Bull's Head' was directed at Beja, another important road junction, and was spearheaded by the bulk of the German armour, including 14 Tigers, 20 PzKpfw IVs and 40 PzKpfw IIIs, led by Oberst Rudolph Lang. It was unfortunate for Lang that his axis of advance had been chosen for him, the route winding along narrow valleys which prevented his tanks from deploying properly; for on 26 February the German column was stopped in its tracks by the little garrison of Sidi Nsir, consisting of 5th Hampshires and 155 Battery Royal Artillery. An epic defence, from which only 120 Hampshires and nine Gunners emerged, cost Lang a complete day, time which was put to good use by the defenders of the main

[1] Holland was awarded the D.S.O., his driver, Tpr. John Mitten the M.M., and Renton the M.C. For a full account of this remarkable episode see the author's *Through mud and Blood*, pp 147-151 (Robert Hale).

British position at Hunt's Gap, several miles in rear. When the German advance was resumed the following day it was confronted by a carefully interlocked defensive front manned by 14th and 24th Hampshires, 2/5th Leicesters, and two squadrons of North Irish Horse Churchills, well supported by medium and field artillery.

Hammered by medium artillery and assailed from the flanks by the fire of anti-tank guns and hull-down Churchills, the Panzers attacked twice, and were beaten back each time with loss. By evening it was clear that the assault had failed, and the North Irish Horse could claim to be the first British armoured regiment to have knocked out a Tiger by direct gunfire.

After 'Ochsenkopf', 1st Army's front became quiet for a while and interest centred on southern Tunisia, where 8th Army was storming the Mareth Line and the Wadi Akarit defences. As the enemy withdrew northwards 1st Army mounted an operation designed to cut them off by forcing the Fondouk Pass and seizing the city of Kairouan on the coastal plain. This took place on 8 April, 51 RTR supporting 128 Hampshire Brigade at nearby Pichon. Having taken their objectives, the

To counter this, many of the vehicles which served in North Africa carried a canvas apron which was slung between the forward horns, as seen on this

'Kingforce' Mark III. Also visible are the ends of the side rails on which a dummy lorry canopy and cab rested before Alamein, and which were later used for stowage.

regiment realized that by exploiting along the hig ground to the south they could take the massiv Djebel Rhorab, which dominated the pass belo with its anti-tank guns. Permission to do this wa refused, with the result that when the Sherman of 17th/21st Lancers tried to batter their wa through later in the day only a handful survive The pass was taken the following day, but by the 1st Italian Army had slipped out of the trap.

The Axis forces were now confined to th north-east corner of the country, and it was full appreciated by both sides that once a gap ha been forced in the mountain defences and th armoured divisions were unleashed into the plai beyond, the campaign would be over. The Medjerd Valley east of Medjez el Bab offered such a ga and it was here that the main effort would b made by the infantry divisions and their supportin armour. In addition to the North Irish Horse an 142 Regiment RAC, the whole of the newl arrived 21 Tank Brigade 12 RTR, 48 RTR an 145 (Duke of Wellington's) Regiment RAC would available for the operation. (A secondary penetratio was to have been effected east of Bou Arada b 46th Division and 51 RTR. This was abandone after some very hard fighting).

North of the river was the notorious Longsto Hill with its twin summits, Djebel Ahmera an Djebel Rhar; to the south a series of ridges rolle away towards the edge of the coastal plain, an round these wound the road leading directly fro Medjez el Bab to Tunis itself. This was the fir time that Churchills had been used en masse i support of a major offensive.

On 21 April the Germans mounted a spoilin attack led by tanks, and succeeded in capturing feature known as Banana Ridge. The attack wa held and turned back by 48 RTR, 142 and 14 Regiments, and by nightfall the ridge was on more in British hands.

Two days later 1st Army's own offensive bega 145 Regiment supporting 24 Guards Brigade on Point 151, while 142 Regiment accompanied Infantry Brigade in its assault on Gueriat Atach. This latter feature was fiercely conteste and changed hands several times. 142 Regimen suffered severely, the commanding officer, Lt-Co

. S. Birkbeck, being killed while leading a desperate
ounter-attack in person. The ridge did not fall
ntil the evening of the following day, after 48
TR and fresh infantry had been brought up.

North of the river, 36 Brigade had captured the
estern peak of Longstop, the Djebel Ahmera; on
3 April. Here the uppermost slopes were too
eep even for Churchills, and the infantry had
uffered cruelly during their climb, 8th Argylls
eing reduced to a total of 40 men by the time
ey reached the crest. Three days later the North
ish Horse supported 5th Buffs in their attack on
jebel Rhar. 'At times whole platoons were
idden by bursting shells, but they pressed on with
agnificent spirit as though taking part in peace-
me manoeuvres. A machine gun post threatened
 hold up the attack, but immediate action by No. 4
roop silenced it and Sgt. O'Hare, climbing high
n the southern side of Point 289, dealt with three
ore such posts. At the head of the saddle between
e Ahmera and the Rhar, Lt. Pope encountered
other machine gun and mortar post, and finally
 75mm gun badly sited to fire down the western

General view of Dieppe beach and sea wall. The damaged tank shows (left to right): the Calgary Regiment's tactical number, recognition panel, squadron and troop marking, and 1st Canadian Army Tank Brigade insignia. Above these the wreckage of the deep wading exhaust is visible.

re-entrant; after one round of 6pdr. and a burst of
Besa the crew surrendered; Sgt. O'Hare then tackled
the ascent and on reaching the summit after a
magnificent climb took over 50 prisoners.'[1]

Longstop had fallen with the loss of only 40
casualties to the Buffs. The captured German
commander commented: 'When it was apparent
that tanks were being used over the high ground,
I knew all was over.'

On 26 April, 24 Guards Brigade, supported by
145 Regiment, took Djebel Asoud and obtained a
precarious toe-hold on Djebel Bou Aoukaz, but was
unable to make further progress. The valley between
the two ridges was known as the Gab Gab Gap and
through this the enemy armour, including a high
proportion of Tigers, launched daily counter-attacks,

[1] *North Irish Horse Battle Report.*

One of the tanks to cross the sea wall was this 'C' Sqn. Mark III carrying an elementary bobbin mat-layer.

requiring the constant presence of 48 RTR, 142 and 145 Regiments to hold the gains already made.

The hold-up at Djebel Bou Aoukaz led to a search for an alternative route through the valley. Such a route could be obtained by the capture of the road junction at Peter's Corner, which was covered by defensive positions at Cactus Farm and Sidi Abdallah. These were unsuccessfully attacked on 28 and 29 April by 12 Brigade, supported by 12 RTR, who lost no less than 36 of their tanks, including several on the objective itself. The German garrison (III Battalion, 5th Fallschirmjäger Regiment) was aided by the fortuitous presence of nine Tigers, but also conducted a most aggressive close-quarter defence with Molotov cocktails and magnetic mines. While they admired the spirit of the British tank men, several of whom they saved from burning vehicles, they felt that the overall planning of this operation had been poor, 12 RTR survivors confirming that little detailed reconnaissance had been carried out.

During the next few days the battle was replanned. On 6 May the advance through the valley was resumed with 4th British Division and 21 Tank Brigade on the right, and 4th Indian Division and 25 Tank Brigade on the left. German resistance was at its last gasp, and by noon the British infantry were digging in on Djebel Bou Aoukaz. Throughout the afternoon 142 Regiment crews watched 7th Armoured Division streaming through the gap and out onto the plain beyond. 'It was a wonderful sight for units of the First Army, who had never yet seen large formations of tanks manoeuvring over open ground after the manner of the Western Desert.'

A week later the war in Africa was over.

ITALY

It would be more than a year before the tank brigades heard another shot fired in anger, most of this time being spent in Algeria, waiting until shipping space could be found to transport them to Italy. They were, therefore, spared the frustration of Cassino; but on 22/23 May 1944, 25 Tank Brigade was engaged with 1st Canadian Division in the breaking of the Hitler Line.

Here, the enemy had spared no pains to make his defence works tank-proof. Natural features were converted into anti-tank ditches, mines were laid, bunkers were constructed and anti-tank guns carefully sited, while behind the lines a counter-attack force of tanks and tank destroyers stood ready to move to any threatened point. In addition new and deadly threat awaited the Churchills the Panther turret, mounted on a concrete casemate at ground level, all but invisible until it opened fire.

The sector chosen for the breakthrough lay between Aquino and Pontecorvo. Following a heavy bombardment the Canadians attacked on 23 May, supported by the entire brigade North Irish Horse on the right, 51 RTR in the centre and 142 Regiment on the left. Intense shelling, mortar and machine gun fire forced the infantry to go to ground as soon as they emerged from close cover, and the Churchills passed through to engage the static defences in a murderous fire-fight which was, in places, conducted at only 400 yards range. Expenditure of ammunition was prodigious, so much so that in one instance cooks, batmen, clerks and lorry drivers brought up fresh supplies under heavy fire, on foot. Gradually the defenders' fire was suppressed and the infantry were able to fight their way through the German position. By nightfall the Hitler Line had been broken and the road to Rome was open, although the cost in tanks had been high.

The Churchills' next involvement in Italy was at the Gothic Line, both tank brigades fighting in support of I Canadian and V British Corps. German fortifications here were very similar to those in the Hitler Line, but in far greater depth and disposed along an apparently endless series of ridges that ran down from the mountains towards the sea. The object of the Allies, once the line had been broken, was to loose their armoured divisions onto the Lombardy Plain beyond, and so possibly end the Italian campaign in 1944.

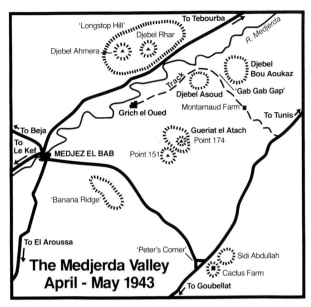

The Medjerda Valley April - May 1943

The battle lasted from 28 August until 17 October. For those involved it was a constant series of tactical problems involving all the weapons of modern war. When one ridge was taken, the only reward was the sight of another ridge beyond, equally well fortified and defended as tenaciously as the last. In a terrain which favoured the defence to such an extent it was inevitable that progress was slow and success uneven. Throughout, the tanks provided the closest possible support for their hard-pressed infantry, the report of 128 Brigade, for example, remarking of the North

Second Lieutenant Appleby's T31665R, a 'Kingforce' Mark III knocked out near Kidney Ridge on 27 October 1942. Details of the damage sustained can be found in the text.

Irish Horse that 'Day after day their Churchills forced positions and supported our infantry over appalling tank country. Undaunted, squadron leaders on foot led their tanks up seemingly impossible slopes. One tank actually slipped over and crashed two hundred feet down a ravine, having turned over six times in its descent.'

To describe the part played by the Churchills would, therefore, be to describe the full course of the battle itself, clearly an impossible task in the space available; but the following incident involving 51 RTR may be taken as typical of the actions which were fought daily along this front.

'On 20 September, 25 Tank Brigade received orders from 4th Division that, as the weather was breaking, an armoured thrust would be made to secure a bridgehead over the River Marrechio before dark. The Regiment was ordered to lead the thrust, and after passing Point 113 on which 'B' Squadron were supporting 1/6th Surreys, 'A' Squadron, attacking two troops up, gained the next ridge. Heavy anti-tank fire then opened up from the left flank but smoke laid by RHQ and 'C' Squadron

tanks gave some valuable cover. Once the valley wa[s] reached the left flank was covered by Point 99, bu[t] an anti-tank gun then opened up from the road o[n] the right. The supporting troops [i.e. the infantry] destroyed this, so enabling the attack to be presse[d] home and yet another objective, Point 213, wa[s] dominated. This very successful operation wa[s] carried out against heavy anti-tank opposition whic[h] knocked out five of 'A' Squadron's tanks and on[e] of 'C' Squadron's. Seven anti-tank positions wer[e] later found to have been destroyed together wit[h] several machine gun positions.'[1]

By the time 8th Army had fought its wa[y] through the Gothic Line, the weather had broke[n] completely and the thickening mud prevente[d] any exploitation across the low-lying plain[s] beyond. During the winter 142 and 145 Regiment[s] were disbanded and 25 Tank Brigade became a[n] armoured engineer formation based on 51 RTR[,] while the North Irish Horse moved across to 2[1] Tank Brigade and several squadrons were traine[d] in the use of the Crocodile (see Variants section).

Mobile operations commenced again on 9 Apri[l] 1945, with 21 Tank Brigade flaming and blastin[g] its way through the enemy's winter defence[s] along the Senio in support of 8th Indian an[d] 2nd New Zealand Divisions. The only obstacl[e]

The Regimental and squadron order of battle of an Infantry Tank Regiment. This organisation is typical of those units involved in the Gothic Line battles in Italy in the autumn of 1944.

[1] *A Short History of the 51st Battalion Royal Tank Regiment.*

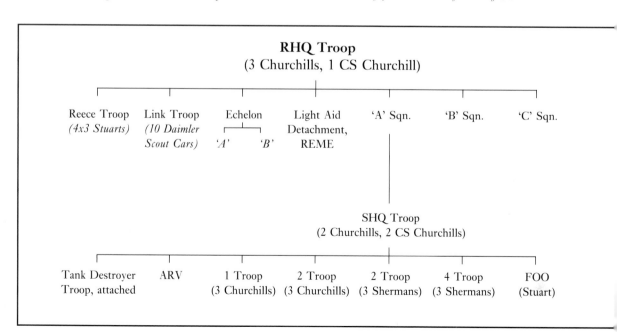

RHQ Troop
(3 Churchills, 1 CS Churchill)

| Reece Troop (4x3 Stuarts) | Link Troop (10 Daimler Scout Cars) | Echelon 'A' 'B' | Light Aid Detachment, REME | 'A' Sqn. | 'B' Sqn. | 'C' Sqn. |

SHQ Troop
(2 Churchills, 2 CS Churchills)

| Tank Destroyer Troop, attached | ARV | 1 Troop (3 Churchills) | 2 Troop (3 Churchills) | 2 Troop (3 Shermans) | 4 Troop (3 Shermans) | FOO (Stuart) |

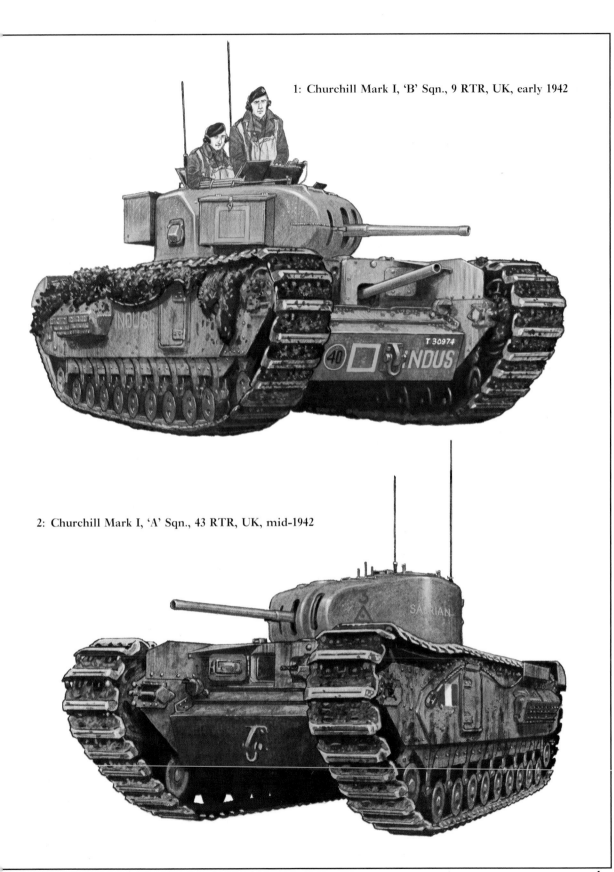

1: Churchill Mark I, 'B' Sqn., 9 RTR, UK, early 1942

2: Churchill Mark I, 'A' Sqn., 43 RTR, UK, mid-1942

A

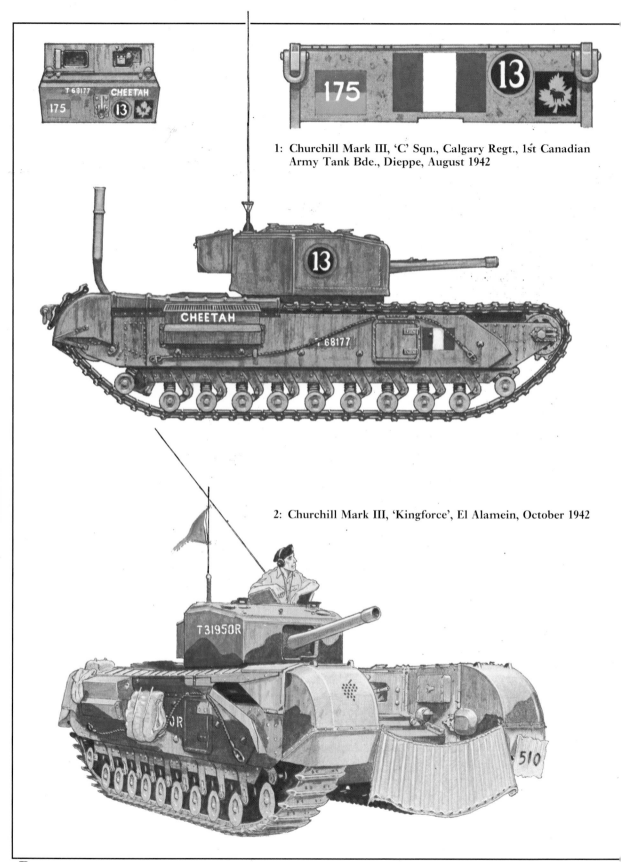

1: Churchill Mark III, 'C' Sqn., Calgary Regt., 1st Canadian Army Tank Bde., Dieppe, August 1942

2: Churchill Mark III, 'Kingforce', El Alamein, October 1942

B

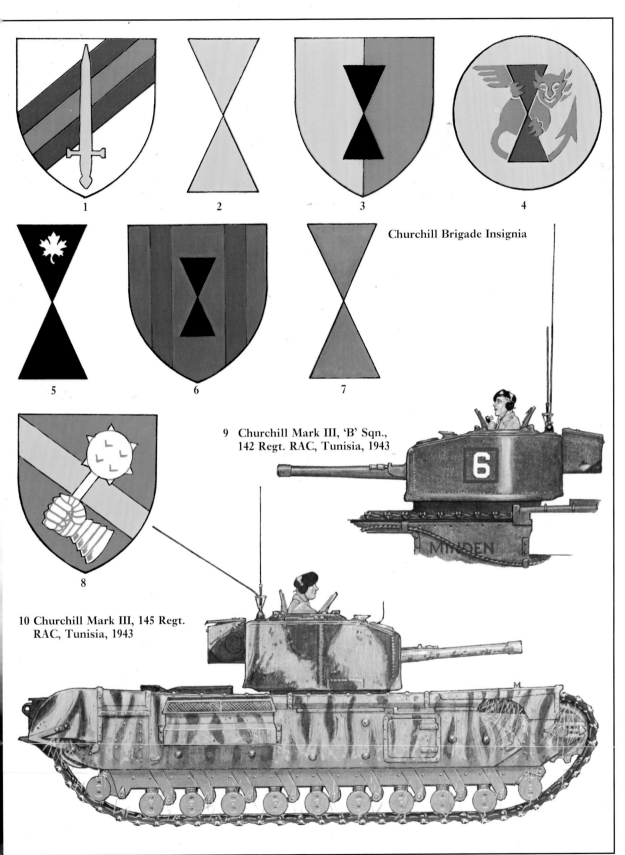

1

2

3

4

Churchill Brigade Insignia

5

6

7

9 Churchill Mark III, 'B' Sqn.,
142 Regt. RAC, Tunisia, 1943

8

10 Churchill Mark III, 145 Regt.
RAC, Tunisia, 1943

C

CHURCHILL MARK III
3rd Scots Guards, 6th Guards Tank Brigade, UK/Normandy 1944

SPECIFICATIONS

Crew: 5
Combat weight: 39 tons kg
Power-to-weight ratio: 8.75 hp/ton
Hull length: 24 ft 5 ins.
Overall length: 24 ft 5 ins.
Height: 8 ft
Width: 10 ft 8 ins.
Engine: Bedford Twin-Six 350 hp
Transmission: Merritt-Brown four-speed gearbox
Steering: Controlled differential
Max. speed (road): 15.5 mph
Max. speed (cross-country): 8 mph

Fording depth: 3 ft 4 ins. (without Preparation)
Vertical obstacle: 2 ft 6 ins.
Armament: 6pdr. Gun (Ordnance QF Mk III)
Main gun ammunition: 6pdr. APC (Armour-piercing with cap)
6pdr. APC, BC (Armour-piercing with cap, Ballistic Cap)
6pdr. APDS (Armour-piercing, discarding sabot)
Muzzle velocity: 2965 ft/sec (APDS)
Armour penetration: 81mm at 500 yds./30 degrees
Stowed main gun rounds: 84
Gun depression/elevation: -12.5 degrees/ +20 degrees

KEY

1. Jack blocks
2. Gear lever and console
3. Binnacle compass
4. Oil Can
5. Driver's periscope
6. Shell stowage
7. Ordnance QF Mk III 6pdr. gun
8. Co-axial Besa machine gun
9. Power traverse
10. Gunner's telescope sight
11. Periscope
12. 2 in. bomb thrower
13. Ventilator
14. Loader/Operator's hatch
15. 6pdr. gun breech
16. 'A'-set aerial
17. Wireless set No.19
18. 'B'-set aerial
19. Commander's seat
20. Fire extinguisher
21. Signal flags
22. Gearbox
23. Left main brake
24. Section through exhaust
25. Bedford Twin-Six 350hp engine
26. Left fuel tanks
27. 20-round magazines for Thompson submachine gun
28. Vehicle serial number
29. Water tank
30. CO_2 cylinder
31. Bren gun ammunition
32. Besa ammunition
33. Bren gun & Thompson SMG (stowed)
34. Besa ammunition
35. Gas capes
36. Left sponson escape hatch
37. Hellensen lamp
38. Red-white-red recognition flash
39. Hull gunner's seat
40. Toolbox
41. Besa ammunition
42. Watertank
43. Handbrake
44. Clutch
45. Foot brake
46. Accelerator
47. Tiller bar
48. Driver's seat

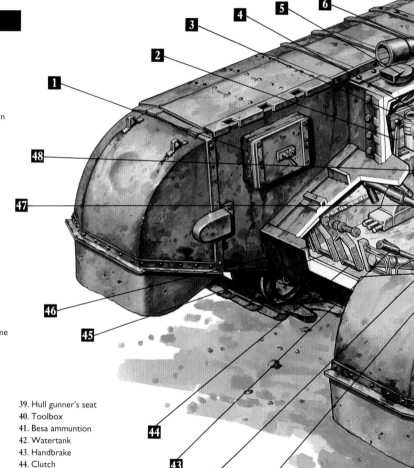

D

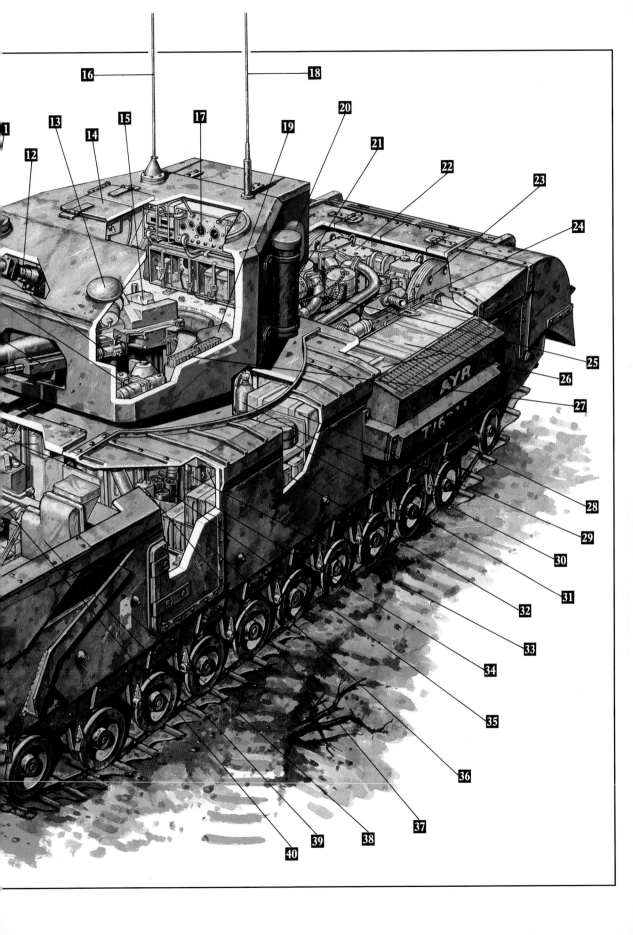

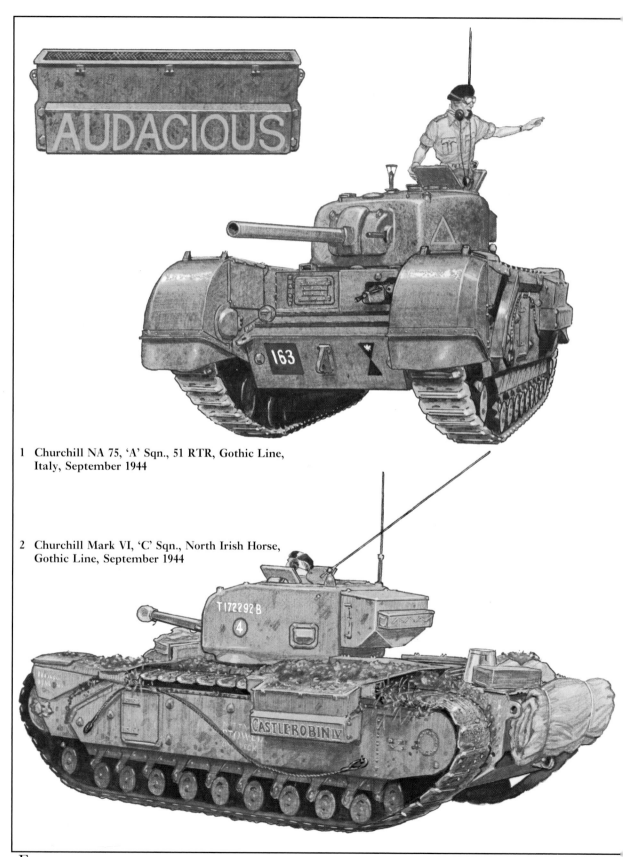

1 Churchill NA 75, 'A' Sqn., 51 RTR, Gothic Line,
Italy, September 1944

2 Churchill Mark VI, 'C' Sqn., North Irish Horse,
Gothic Line, September 1944

E

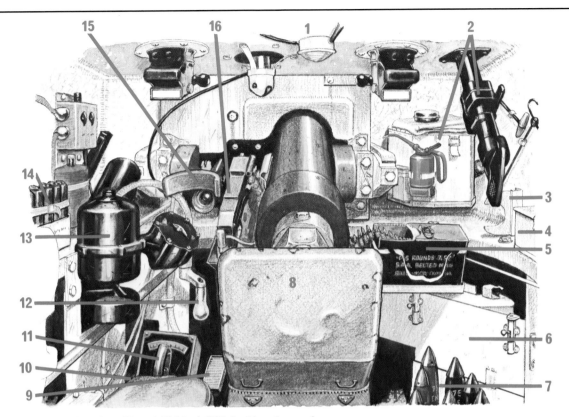

Top: Turret interior, Churchill Mark VII, looking forward
Bottom: Interior of forward hull positions, Churchill Crocodile. See Key on page 46.

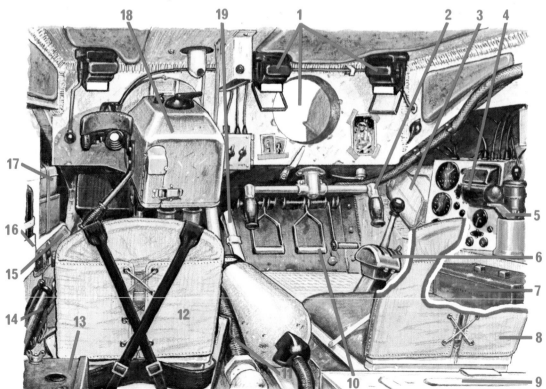

F

1 Trooper, 107 Regt. RAC, Reichswald, February 1945
2 Lance-corporal, 'C' Sqn., 7 RTR, Korea, winter 1950-51

(a)–(f) Ammunition types–see Plates commentary for details

G

Tanks of Nos 7 and 8 Troops No 2 Squadron 4th Grenadier Guards photographed in Holland during the autumn of 1944. Troop names began with K and the nearest vehicle, a Mark IV, has KINGSTON stencilled on the air intake. On the second vehicle the unit number 152 on a red square above a white bar can be seen on the stern plate, with the troop number 7 on the turret stowage bin above. The leading tank, a Mark VI, has GLOUCESTER stencilled on the air intake and belonged to 8 Troop, which named its vehicles with the initial letter G.

now remaining between 8th Army and the Po Valley was the heavily defended Argenta Gap between Lake Comacchio and the River Reno, but this was stormed on 18 April in a dashing operation carried out by 48 RTR and 36 Brigade. With their last defence line gone, the Germans' front collapsed and even the slow Churchills joined in the general pursuit which took place before the final surrender on 2 May 1945.

NORTH-WEST EUROPE

The Churchill-based variants of 79th Armoured Division apart, the first Infantry Tank formation to serve in Normandy was 31 Tank Brigade (7 and 9 RTR), which was committed to action on 26 June in support of 15th (Scottish) Division.

(The third regiment in 31 Brigade was 141 (The Buffs) Regiment RAC, a Crocodile unit which was committed as required along the front. 7 RTR was in fact the renumbered 10th, the original Seventh having been lost at Tobruk in 1942). During the days that followed the line was pushed steadily southwards until by 10th July the Odon had been crossed and 7 RTR were preparing to assault Hill 112 with 43rd (Wessex) Division.

The hill set about earning its evil reputation at once. 'C' Squadron and 5th Somerset Light Infantry were shelled mercilessly as they climbed the slopes within sight of the German armour, and the attack stalled with severe loss.[1] It was resumed later in the day by 'A' Squadron and 5th Duke of Cornwall's Light Infantry, and this time succeeded, although during the night the DCLI were counter-attacked no less than fourteen times by Tigers and Panzer-Grenadiers, incurring 240 casualties and the loss of all their anti-tank guns.

On 15 July, 34 Tank Brigade (107 (King's Own), 147 (Hampshire) and 153 (Essex) Regiments RAC) moved into the line and began a series of heavy raids against selected enemy positions in conjunction with 15th Division. 107 Regiment attacked Le Bon Repos and Esquay, and 153 Regiment captured Gavrus and Bougy the following day, beating off a furious counterattack by Tigers, Panthers and Panzer Grenadiers. During this action the Essex lost twelve Churchills and incurred a total of 96 personnel casualties, of whom 39 were killed. Among the wounded was the regiment's Commanding Officer, Lt.Col. Wood, and 153 was taken over by Maj. Norris King, who, it will be recalled, had commanded 'Kingforce' at Alamein.[2]

On 17 July, 147 Regiment raided Evrecy; on 23 July, 107 was back at Esquay; and on 2 August the raids reached their climax with 107 at Esquay again, 147 at Bougy and 153 at Maltot, which had also been raided by 7 RTR. The object of these raids was to tie down the German armour along the British sector of the front and so prevent it

[1] Officer casualties were extremely high in Normandy due to the cover provided for Snipers by the bocage. In this one action 7 RTR l lost its CO, 2i/c and three Troop leaders; in six weeks' fighting the regiment lost a total of 36 officers.
[2] A fictional but accurate account of this engagement is contained in the late Maj. John Foley's Death of a Regiment.

T31950R, commanded by Second Lieutenant Howard, was badly damaged at Tel el Aqqaqir on 3 November 1942. The tank 'came under heavy 50mm fire and two shots close together on the left sprocket broke the track and removed two seven-toothed segments from the wheel. The 6pdr. was rendered useless by a shot and the front Besa cover bent over. An HE shell knocked off the cupola door smashing the periscope' – extract from 'Kingforce' Report. (Colonel P. W. H. Whitely, O.B.E. T.D.)

from interfering with the Americans' break-out from the beachhead; and they are of some tactical interest in that the Churchills sometimes towed the infantry's 17pdr. anti-tank guns during the attack, so that a firm defensive front could be established as soon as the objective had been reached.

Meanwhile, 15th (Scottish) Division had moved to the Caumont sector, its place in the line being taken by 53rd (Welsh) Division on 18 July. At Caumont the division had been ordered to mount an attack southwards to secure Hill 309, the western end of the Mont Pincon range, possession of which would further embarrass any German attempt to contain the American break-out. For this operation 15th Division would have the support of the newly arrived 6th Guards Tank Brigade (4th Bn. Grenadier Guards, 4th Bn. Coldstream Guards and 3rd Bn. Scots Guards), with which it had carried out much of its training in England.

The attack went in on 30 July and immediately broke through the thin defensive crust of 326. Infantry Division, which was tired, under strength and had only recently arrived for a rest on what was considered to be a quiet sector. This unfortunate formation suddenly found itself confronted by 174 Churchills, several Crocodiles from 141 Regiment, and a first-class, battlehardened Scots infantry division. The break-in phase was carried out by the Grenadiers, and as soon as this had been completed the Coldstream passed through on the right and the Scots on the left. Soon the tanks were outstripping the infantry, and permission was given for them to advance independently in order to keep up with the timed artillery programme. Little resistance could be offered to this flood of armour and by 1415hrs both regiments were in position on the start line for the final phase of the operation. However, the infantry were still far behind; and it was decided to modify the original plan so that while the Scots protected the left flank of the advance, the Coldstream would take Hill 309 alone, and the Grenadiers would ferry an infantry battalion forward on their Churchills. The plan worked, and during the early evening the Coldstream's tanks crawled onto the summit of the hill, which had been hastily abandoned by the enemy. (At about the same time the Scots Guards were dramatically counter-attacked by *Jagdpanthers* but succeeded in holding their ground.

Caumont was the most concentrated 'I' tank attack of the war, and if the rule book had been thrown away, the end had justified the means. It had taken a day to cover six miles across-country over close bocage, a feat which many felt could only have been performed by Churchills.

During the next three weeks the tank brigades fought in support of the infantry divisions which formed the northern shoulder of the steadily contracting Falaise Pocket, and witnessed the final disintegration of the German field army in France. In 34 Tank Brigade, 153 Regiment was disbanded to make up casualties in the other regiments, and 7 and 9 RTR joined from 31 Tank Brigade, which became a Crocodile formation under 79 Armoured

The Medjerda Valley, scene of the Churchills' first   *committal en masse.*

Division. (7 RTR converted to Crocodiles early in 1945, joining 141 Regiment and 1st Fife and Forfar Yeomanry in 31 Tank Brigade.)

On 10 September, 34 Tank Brigade – less 7 Regiment – supported 45th (West Riding) and 51st (Highland) Divisions in the assault on Le Havre, a strange battle complicated by crowds of French civilians who turned out to welcome their liberators. The garrison commander, Oberst Wildemuth, surrendered to Lt. Kit Bland of 7 RTR from his bed, which also contained his mistress; a nice touch of formality was added to the proceedings by the Oberst having pinned his medals to his pyjamas.

October 1944 found both Churchill brigades fighting in the Low Countries, 6th Guards Tank Brigade capturing Tilburg with 15th Division on the 27th; both formations then moved east immediately to seal off a penetration made by German armour and parachutists in the overextended front held by the US 7th Armored Division. The Guards and 15th Division formed a long-standing partnership which developed its own recognizable tactical style, the hallmark of which was the converging attack by brigades onto a major objective.

To the west operations were in hand to clear the southern shore of the Scheldt estuary, and 34 Tank Brigade were ordered to form a Churchill-based battle group for deep penetration of the enemy's defences. This included 107 Regiment, 49 Divisional Recce Regiment, a troop of Fife and Forfar Yeomanry Crocodiles, 191 Field Regiment RA, 'D' Company 1st Leicestershire, a troop of tank destroyers and two sections of engineers, to which were added later 7th Duke of Wellington's Regiment, 1/4th King's Own Yorkshire Light Infantry, and two further troops of tank destroyers. This unusual formation, known as Clarke-force after the commander of 34 Tank Brigade, moved off on 20 October, after 9 RTR and 56 Brigade had broken the enemy's front; and in ten days it advanced 25 miles, its right flank being covered by 147 Regiment fighting in support of the US 10th ('Timberwolf') Division, and later by 9 RTR. This was accomplished at a cost to 107 Regiment of only 9 killed, 32 wounded and 19 tanks damaged, of which all but two Churchills and four Stuarts were repairable; in exchange the regiment destroyed eight self-propelled guns and took 230 prisoners.

After various minor operations in the Maastricht Appendix and along the German border at Geilenkirchen, 6th Guards and 34 Tank Brigades began concentrating in great secrecy near Nijmegen for Operation 'Veritable', the storming of the Reichswald Forest sector of the Siegfried Line. This began on 8 February 1945 after a bombardment twice as heavy as that fired at El Alamein. On the right, 107 Regiment supported 51st Division along the southern edge of the forest; in the centre, 9 RTR and 147 Regiment fought their way through the forest itself with 53rd Division; and on the left the entire 6th Guards Tank Brigade advanced with 15th Division north of the trees to capture Cleve. The battle was fought in torrential rain and deep mud, in which the only vehicles which managed to remain mobile were the Churchills.

The Reichswald was eight miles deep and varied in width between three and a half and five miles. The German High Command considered it to be completely impassable to tanks and as a result the Siegfried line defences in this sector of the front were hardly more than a line on a map. 'During the night of 8/9 February 9 RTR carried out a fighting advance of 2,000 yards with 160 Infantry Brigade to capture the Stoppelberg feature. This manoeuvre had been thought out and practised a fortnight previously. Moving on a single squadron front, tanks crashed through areas of young plantation and were guided on foot where trees were too solid to smash; but they arrived on the objective, up with their infantry, to whom their noisy

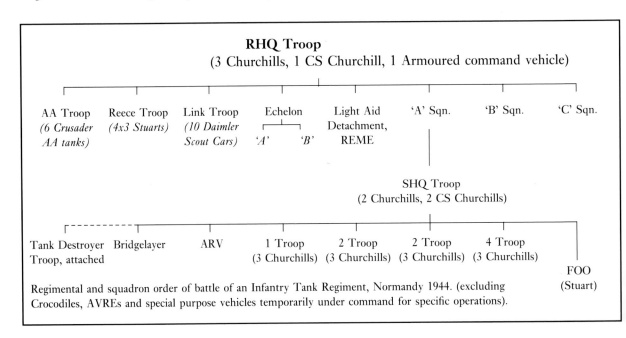

Regimental and squadron order of battle of an Infantry Tank Regiment, Normandy 1944. (excluding Crocodiles, AVREs and special purpose vehicles temporarily under command for specific operations).

BURMA AND KOREA

On 28 April 1945 a solitary Churchill joined 3rd Carabiniers near Allanmyo for field trials. At that time the regiment's much faster Lees were spearheading XXXIII Corps' drive on Rangoon, and it is difficult to see how the vehicle could have been integrated into the operational pattern. There is no record of its being engaged, but its journey forward cannot have been without interest, since there were now more Japanese behind the Carabiniers than in front of them.

Churchills did, however, see action in the Far East. On the outbreak of the Korean War it was decided to add a Crocodile squadron to the establishment of 25th Infantry Brigade Group, the British contingent of the United Nations force. The vehicles were drawn from parks in Germany and manned by 'C' Squadron 7 RTR, who disembarked at Pusan on 15 November 1950.

The majority of the tanks moved north by rail, but one troop made the journey by road, establishing a Churchill record by covering 200 miles on its tracks. The squadron reached the front at the height of the Chinese offensive, and during subsequent

Mark III and Mark I of the North Irish Horse on Longstop Hill; note the rolled anti-dust aprons slung across the bow plates. 'The method by which tanks moved in echelon along the hillside with those higher up moving ahead of those in the valley enabled anti-tank guns to be engaged before they were able to fire on the tanks in the valley' – N.I.H. Battle Report

movement had been comforting and helpful in traversing dense woodland full of disorganized enemy troops. The German Sector Commander, a full colonel, was captured in the melee at first light and protested vigorously that such a use of tanks was "not fair" !'[1]

The Battle of the Reichswald was one of the bitterest fought on the Western Front and it took six days of hard fighting to clear the forest. The whole axis of advance swung south, 15th and 51st Divisions taking Goch on 19 February with support from 6th Guards Tank Brigade, while 34 Tank Brigade fought its way through the Broedersbosch with 52nd (Lowland) Division. Operation 'Veritable' was the last major battle fought by the tank brigades, and succeeded in breaking the enemy's resistance west of the Rhine. When the Rhine was crossed 6th Guards Tank Brigade advanced with the US 17th Airborne Division to capture Munster, and several Crocodile sub-units were still in action when Germany surrendered on 8 May.

[1] *The story of 34 Armoured Brigade (sic).*

'C' Squadron, 51 RTR with men and carriers of the Hampshire Regiment during the Pichon/Fondouk battle.

*Churchills and infantry
moving up to the Gothic Line.*

operations dropped all but one of its trailers and fought as gun tanks, there being no opportunity for flaming while the general situation remained fluid.

On 3 January 1951, 1st Royal Northumberland Fusiliers was heavily attacked and three of its companies cut off. After a difficult approach march through a defile on a narrow, ice-covered track, 5 Troop and two SHQ tanks put in an attack with the regiment's fourth rifle company. 'It proved very successful and two companies were relieved and the third able to break out at last light. Casualties suffered by the infantry during the counter-attack were extremely light owing to the high rate of fire put down by the tanks. It is estimated that the enemy suffered about 150 casualties.'[1]

The UN Forces were now involved in the general retreat known as the 'Pusan Handicap', and 'C' Squadron was ordered south as quickly as possible, crossing the Han River in darkness early on 4 January and arriving at Sangwhan on the 7th, where the withdrawal ended. On the way one Crocodile

[1] *Korean Diary 1950-51, C Squadron 7 RTR.*

had been blown up since it was beyond local repair, and an ARV had been burned when a bridge was blown ahead of it.

However, by the middle of the month the position had been stabilized and the line was beginning to move north again. On 20 January 'C' Squadron came under American control for three weeks, supporting the advance of several Regimental Combat Teams, including the 27th ('Wolfhounds'), 35th and 24th, the first two creating a most favourable impression by their efficiency, the third less so; these operations culminated in the capture of Yongdungpo. Latterly 5 Troop had been harassed by the fire of a captured Cromwell from across the Han, but this was destroyed by a troop of Centurions from 8th King's Royal Irish Hussars. (The Cromwell had originally belonged to 8th Hussars' Recce Troop, which had been ambushed and overwhelmed by human wave tactics in an area known as Compo Valley.)

'C' Squadron rejoined 25th Brigade on 12 February after a road march of 50 miles. The brigade was also closing up to the Han and was having to clear the enemy from every hill along the route, the Churchills providing direct gunfire support as the infantry stormed the slopes. Some long-range shooting was also carried out, 7 Troop engaging targets at a range of 6000 yards.

Following its relief on 21 February the squadron was able to carry out some much-needed maintenance, and did not become operational again until the Chinese launched a fresh offensive on 22 April. On this occasion the Churchills were not so closely engaged; but the ARV, on loan to 8th Hussars, performed prodigies recovering tanks and dismantling road blocks under fire. Once the new threat had been contained a long period of comparative inactivity followed in which the Churchill troops were detailed to stand by in a counter-infiltration role or to act as bridge guards. Peace talks began on 8 July, and three months later the squadron left Korea, having been highly praised by the commander of I Corps, Maj.-Gen. John W. O'Daniel, US Army, for its part in the campaign, particularly during the defeat of the Communist New Year Offensive.

In Korea the Churchills operated under extreme conditions, 47 degrees of frost being recorded at the height of their involvement. Such cold froze tracks to the ground and affected metal: strangely track pins became brittle and cracked, but were held together by ice for long periods. The frozen semi-tundra also prevented the Churchills from exercising their legendary hill-climbing ability, as they could not obtain a tractive grip on such a surface. On the whole, however, the tanks stood up well to the climate in spite of the long marches on their tracks, which exceeded those previously carried out by Churchill units for a comparable period. 'C' Squadron 7 RTR was the last British unit to take Churchills into action; but the vehicle continued to serve with the Irish Army in a much modified form until the late 1960s.

VARIANTS

The Churchill Crocodile is, perhaps, the world's most famous flame-throwing tank. It was developed from trials carried out with Valentines in 1942, and employed pressurized nitrogen as a flame propellant. The basic vehicle was the

Carefully sited Panther turrets on concrete casemates were encountered in the Hitler and Gothic Lines.

Generally they were better concealed than this example, and only disclosed their position when opening fire.

An AVRE attracts curious stares from the crew of a 48 RTR Churchill Mark IV. Specialized armour was

employed later in the Italian campaign than in North-West Europe.

Mark VII, to which was coupled a two-wheeled armoured trailer containing the flaming liquid. From the coupling a pipe led under the tank's belly to emerge into the driving compartment where it joined the flame gun, which occupied the space usually containing the hull machine

gun. On leaving the flame gun the fluid was ignited electrically and threw a jet up to 120 yards, the blazing liquid clinging tenaciously to anything it touched. As the propellant gas steadily lost pressure to a point where the flame gun became inoperable, it was necessary for crews to 'pressure up' their trailers immediately before going into action.

The Crocodile was a terrible weapon; but if the death it inflicted was inhuman, it was no more so than the system against which it fought. On balance it saved lives, for often the mere appearance of a Crocodile was sufficient to frighten the garrison of a strongpoint into surrender; on the other hand, there were plenty of suicidal fanatics who unwisely chose to take their chances. The vehicle was feared and hated by the enemy, whose antitank gunners generally tried to disable the trailer before it could be brought into flaming range; in some instances Crocodile crews who fell into German hands were murdered on the spot. Once empty or if damaged, it was possible to jettison the trailer while the parent vehicle continued to fight as a conventional gun tank. A more rudimentary and less efficient Churchill flame-thrower, the 'Oke', was used by the Calgary Regiment at Dieppe in 1942. The Crocodile saw active service in North-West Europe and Italy, sometimes as part of an assault engineer combat team, and sometimes in direct support of infantry operations against fixed defences. A Crocodile squadron was also despatched to Korea in 1950.

Whilst assault engineering does not in itself form a part of this study, it is necessary to mention that the obvious adaptability of the Churchill's hull, its roomy interior and heavy armour made it eminently suitable for conversion to this role, and it formed the basis of a variety of special-purpose vehicles.

Of these the most famous was the AVRE (Assault Vehicle Royal Engineers), which carried a specially designed turret containing a 290mm muzzle-loading spigot mortar. This weapon threw a 40lb bomb known as 'General Wade's Flying Dustbin', and was used to crack open concrete fortifications. Reloading was carried out through a sliding hatch above the co-driver's seat. The AVRE's construction and standardized fittings permitted the vehicle to be used in a number of ways. It could carry a large fascine which could be dropped into an anti-tank ditch; a small boxgirder bridge which could surmount a sea wall and so provide a means of egress from an invasion beach; and also a bobbin which unrolled a mat ahead of the vehicle, so producing a firm track over areas of soft going.

In addition to the box-girder bridge carried by the AVRE, a turretless bridgelayer was also developed. This carried a 30-foot bridge which was launched by hydraulic arms over the bows and which could carry vehicles up to 60 tons in weight. As well as its more obvious use for crossing small streams, this bridge was also used to reinforce cratered roads. By the end

The Normandy bocage provided ideal cover for snipers, and casualties among tank commanders were high; steel helmets were worn constantly because of this menace *which also required a high degree of vigilance from the infantry, seen here escorting a 7 RTR vehicle through some very close country. Note the heavy external stowage.*

of the war most Churchill regiments included several in their establishment. The Churchill bridgelayer remained in service for some years after the gun tank had been withdrawn.

For crossing larger obstacles a vehicle known as the Ark was developed. This was simply a turretless Churchill hull with folding ramps at either end, which was driven bodily into the obstacle to form a bridge, and temporarily abandoned. If a particular obstacle such as an anti-tank ditch was too deep for one Ark to fill, a second could be driven onto its back, and a series of Arks joined end to end could form a causeway across a shallow river.

Other assault engineering vehicles included an assortment of mine-clearing devices, including rollers, ploughs and projected explosive hose, but none were quite as effective as the Sherman Crab. There were also a number of frames mounting demolition charges which could be attached to the front of a Churchill and placed against concrete fortifications for remote detonation after the carrying vehicle had retired; these went by the names of 'Carrot', 'Onion' and 'Goat', and like the majority of Churchill special-purpose derivatives, stemmed directly from the experience gained during the Dieppe raid.

The Churchill ARV (Armoured Recovery Vehicle) appeared in two versions, the first of which utilized a turretless Mark I or II hull on which a jib had been fitted. The second employed a Mark III or IV hull with the turret replaced by a fixed superstructure mounting a dummy gun, and in addition to a more sophisticated jib was equipped with a two-speed winch and a ground spade.

Somewhat outside the mainstream of Churchill development was the 3in. Gun Carrier. This vehicle was designed at the end of 1941 to utilize stocks of the obsolete 3in. anti-aircraft gun in the role subsequently undertaken by the tank destroyer in infantry/tank operations. However, the Gun Carrier was a crude extemporization in which the gun was mounted in the tank's front

The 30-foot bridge carried by the Churchill bridgelayer *was also used to reinforce cratered roads.*

plate with traverse limited to five degrees right and left of centre, surmounted by an 88mm fixed superstructure. Only 24 of these vehicles were built, and they were subsequently converted to other uses.

THE PLATES

Plate A1: *Churchill Mark I of 'B' Squadron, 9th Royal Tank Regiment during training in the United Kingdom, early 1942*
The overall colour scheme is the medium grey sometimes called 'factory finish'. At this stage 9 RTR was the second senior regiment of 31 Tank Brigade; they followed RTR tradition in naming tanks with the initial letter coinciding with their regimental number (e.g. 'I', the ninth letter of the alphabet); and normal practice, in marking squadron signs and names in yellow as second senior regiment. The square of 'B' Sqn. is marked on the turret bin and front plate, and the name *Indus* on the front plate and hull sides. A bridge classification number in black within a yellow ring is carried on the off-side of the front plate, and the serial number T30974 on the nearside. Much of the mud carried up onto the top run of the track will inevitably fall away, marking the hull with broad vertical streaks. The difference in size between the turret-mounted 2pdr. and the 3in. howitzer in the hull is clearly evident.

Plate A2: *Churchill Mark I of 'A' Squadron, 43rd Royal Tank Regiment during training in the United Kingdom, mid-1942*
Essentially similar to A1 above, this vehicle has a Besa machine gun in place of the 3in. howitzer in the hull. This version has sometimes been called 'Mark II', although it is generally accepted that the Mark II was a Close Support development of the Mark I in which the 2pdr. and 3in. howitzer were simply transposed.

Details of this vehicle are taken from a contemporary colour photograph. At this period 43 RTR formed part of 33 Tank Brigade, the third brigade of the 3rd (Mixed) Division; but it later became the experimental regiment of 75th Armoured Division. The finish is an overall khaki brown, not unlike the colour of British battledress; this 'Standard

Of all the types of AFV captured, the Panther seemed to appeal most to Churchill crews, possibly because it was so different from their own vehicles. The 4th Coldstream *employed one, named* **Cuckoo,** *seen here during the fighting in the Maastricht Appendix; and in Italy 1945 Regiment RAC used another called* **Deserter.**

Camouflage Colour No. 2' was used by several UK-based units at this time. Heavy going has coated the hull with mud, but the red/white/red recognition flash is still visible forward of the sponson hatch. Tank names in 43 RTR began with 'S' – the Territorial battalions numbered 40–51 naturally could not follow the traditional RTR letter/number sequence – and the name *Saurian* appears on the turret side in yellow; immediately ahead of it is a slightly unusual squadron internal code, the red triangle containing a red dot with, presumably, the troop number above. For some reason the commander's sighting vanes on the turret roof are also red, though this probably would not have survived on active service.

Plate B1: *Churchill Mark III of 'C' Squadron, Calgary Regiment, 1st Canadian Army Tank Brigade; Dieppe raid, 19 August 1942*
Few units have gone into action with their tanks as lavishly marked as the Calgarys at Dieppe; and after studying numerous photographs, including some colour film taken on the beach, we have selected *Cheetah*, a Mark III which is known to have crossed the sea wall and fought in the ornamental gardens beyond, slugging it out with German gun positions in the houses on the seafront. Overall finish is Middle Bronze Green, and the side-view shows, from hull front to rear, the red/white/red flash ahead of the sponson door; the serial T68177 between the door and the air intake, in white; and the name in white on the upper air intake. On the turret side is the 'C' Sqn. circle, in French grey, round a black back-

9 RTR lying up with their infantry just before the start of the Reichswald battle. The barked stakes alongside the track are an aid to night driving. The battle was fought in torrential rain, witness the waterproof tanksuit and the temporary air louvre cover.

ground for the white troop number '13' . The left-hand detail shows the bow plate with (left to right) the Canadian 'I' tank unit marking, a square of dark green over ochre, with the regimental number '175' superimposed; the serial; the squadron/troop marking repeated from the turret; the 1st Canadian Army Tank Brigade symbol of a black ram on a yellow maple leaf on a black square; and the name. The hull rear plate (right-hand detail) bears the Infantry Tank marking and regimental number; the recognition flash; the squadron/troop markings; and the brigade sign. The deep wading vents are painted black, with some heat discoloration.

Plate B2: *Churchill Mark III of 'Kingforce';* *El Alamein, October 1942*

Commanded by 2nd Lt. Howard, this tank was badly damaged on 3 November. The overall finish of sand yellow is camouflaged with disruptive patches of dark blue-grey – probably the colour 'Slate Grey No. 34'. The serial T31950R is painted aft of the sponson door, on the turret side and on the near-side of the bow plate. The apparent marking in the shape of a 'bunch of grapes' on the front of the off-side track guard is not thought to have any significance, although seen on at least two of the Churchills of Kingforce'; it may well be a legacy of the fitting of the dummy 'lorry tilt' device. 'Kingforce' was given the tactical number '510', scrawled in black on a piece of cardboard and fastened to the front of the nearside track guard; but this is seldom seen in photos. The use of the apron slung between the track horns is described in the text. They were generally construed of heavy canvas with chestnut paling 'splints'.

A Churchill Mark V in close woodland. 'We had never thought that anyone in their right mind would use tanks in this forest; it is most unfair' – German sector commander during Operation 'Veritable'.

Plate C: *Churchill Brigade Insignia*
1: 6th Guards Tank Bde. **2:** 21 Army Tank Bde., original style. **3:** 21 Tank Bde., intermediate style. **4:** 21 Tank Bde., final style. The diabolo could be in black or dark blue, and sometimes the yellow disc was omitted. **5:** 25 Tank Bde. The maple leaf was added to the brigade's black diabolo as a compliment from 1st Canadian Infantry Division after the Hitler Line fighting in May 1944. **6:** 25 Armoured Engineer Bde., in RE colours with the black diabolo commemorating its Infantry Tank origins. **7:** 31 Tank Bde. – seldom visible in monochrome photos, as the grass green diabolo does not show up against the background khaki green. The brigade's two regiments, 7 and 9 RTR. can often be identified by their prominent tactical numbers, '991' and '992'. **8:** 34 Tank Bde.

Plate C9: *Churchill Mark III, 'B' Squadron, 142 (Suffolk) Regiment RAC; Tunisia, early 1943*
The overall colour is a weathered Middle Bronze Green, but later in the campaign the Suffolks deliberately dappled this with local mud. Being the junior regiment of its brigade, the 142nd marked in blue. The 'B' Squadron square on the turret and the name *Minden* behind the sponson

door are in this colour, with a white troop number '6' inside the former. No other markings seem to have been visible on this vehicle.

Plate C10: *Churchill Mark III, 145 (Duke of Wellington's) Regiment RAC; Tunisia, 1943*
The 'Duke's' also used local mud to break up their outlines, but appear to have preferred a tigerstripe pattern. The junior regiment of 21 Tank Brigade, the 145th would have marked in blue, but all insignia have been obscured here apart from a blue 'C' on the side of the turret bin.

Plate D: *Churchill Mark III of No 1 Troop, Right Flank Squadron, 3rd Scots Guards, 6th Guards Tank Brigade, UK/Normandy 1944*
Despite the fact that, for the sake of convenience, the inner hull wall and top run of the tracks have been omitted, thereby permitting a wider view inside the vehicle, the first impression received by the reader is that the interior is impossibly cramped; yet, by the standards of the day, the Churchill was considered roomy and its crew were able to stow most of their personal kit inside, unlike those of other tanks.

Closest to the viewpoint is the driving compartment, showing the driver's and hull-gunner's seat and the driving controls; further details of the last can be found on Plate F2. For obvious reasons the hull-gunner's Besa machine gun and mounting are not shown. Immediately behind and to the left of the driver's seat is an ammunition stowage bin with cruciform metal safety clips still attached to the base of the rounds.

Behind the driving compartment is the fighting compartment surmounted by the turret. In action the gunner's eye remained fixed to his telescopic gunsight, with his forehead resting on the brow-pad above. Above this is a 'mushroom' ventilator which, despite its fan, was never able to clear the turret of cordite fumes when closed down. Across the turret to the left is a 2in bomb-thrower. This was capable of firing smoke grenades which could be used to create a screen concealing the vehicle from the enemy and allowing the tank to safely withdraw from serious trouble. The spent case deflector shield, intended to intercept the hot shell

ases as they were ejected violently from the main rmament breech on recoil, then deflect them to the urret floor, has been omitted so that full details of he radio equipment can be shown in the turret ustle.

Beyond the turret are the engine and transmission/ inal drive compartments. In order to clearly depict letails of the latter , neither the bulkhead separating he two compartments nor the intermediate fan ave been shown, although the position of both an be clearly seen in the drawing on p.4.

The positions of the various markings, i.e. brigade nsignia, unit tactical number, bridge classification, rdnance number, squadron marking and vehicle ame, were standard throughout the regiment. The 3rd Scots Guards' tank squadrons were amed Right Flank, 'S' and Left Flank, marked espectively on vehicles with the conventional A, 3 and C Squadron symbols.

Eagle, an RHQ tank of 4th Coldstream Guards, ferrying men of the US 17th Airborne Division during the advance across Westphalia.

Plate E1: *Churchill NA 75 of 'A' Squadron, 51 RTR; Gothic Line, Italy, September 1944*

This particular vehicle which is known to have been commanded by Lieutenant Jim Massey, is in an overall finish of well-worn Middle Bronze Green; as 51 RTR were the second regiment in their brigade the 'A' Squadron triangle on the turret and the name *Audacious* on the lower air intake are in yellow. The regimental number '163' can be seen in rounded white digits on the off-side of the bow plate; the background is a faded brown square, legacy of the Mixed Division days. The 25 Tank Brigade sign was carried on the near-side end of the bow plate. The NA 75 was equipped with the Sherman 75mm gun.

6 Troop, 'C' Squadron, 7 RTR in Compo Valley, Korea. As there was no opportunity for flaming, the *Crocodiles usually dropped their trailers and fought as gun tanks. (Major B. H. S. Clarke, RTR)*

4 Three hand grenades
5 Box of Besa ammunition in feed tray
6 Right pannier shell bin, with total of 26 rounds HE and AP 75mm shot, and four rounds smoke. Below bin stowage for six tins of ration biscuits.
7 Fourteen rounds 75mm shot, HE and AP mixed
8 75mm gun, with empty case deflector and empty case ba at breech
9 Gunner's firing pedal
10 Gunner's seat
11 Spade grip of power traverse controls
12 Hand traverse
13 Power traverse
14 Ten 20-round magazines for Thompson SMG; or eight 32-round magazines for Sten, if carried instead
15 Gunner's telescope sight
16 Besa machine gun, with deflector, chute, and spen cartridge bin

Plate E2: *Churchill Mark VI of 'C' Squadron, North Irish Horse; Gothic Line, Italy, September 1944*

Photographed towards the end of the Gothic Line fighting, this Mark VI is heavily weathered and its overall Bronze Green is badly faded. As senior regiment in their brigade the North Irish Horse should have marked in red, but the 'C' Squadron circle on the turret certainly appears to be in blue, around a white troop number '4'. This may be one of those cases where Royal Armoured Corps regiments marked their squadrons by seniority e.g. red for 'A', yellow for 'B', and blue for 'C'. The name on the lower air intake, *Castlerobin IV*, seems to be in faded red or Ulster orange, trimmed thinly with white. The white serial T172292R can be seen high on the turret, and faded shipping stencils on the hull sides. The tank tarpaulin is strapped across the vacant rear hull brackets for the external fuel tank, and for personal stowage an old ammunition box has been welded to the turret bustle.

Plate F1: *Interior view of a Churchill Mark VII turret, looking forward*

The perspective has necessarily been distorted slightly, to allow more clarity.

Key;
1 Light
2 2in. bomb thrower, and stowage for twenty smoke bombs
3 Cartridge extractor

Plate F2: *Interior view of a Churchill Mark VII/Crocodile hull*

The painting, slightly 'opened out' laterally for clarity, shows the driver's and flame gunner's positions in a Crocodile. The driver's seat back has been 'cut away' to expose more of his controls it was of the same construction as the gunner's seat. Apart from the substitution of the flame gun and its cylinders and hoses for the Besa machine gun, there was no difference between these positions and those of a Mark VII gun tank.

Key;
1 Driver's periscopes; and direct vision port, open
2 Tiller bar
3 Stowage for two haversacks, anti-gas capes and gloves, etc
4 Driver's instrument panel
5 Binnacle compass
6 Gear lever and console
7 Box with spare periscope prisms and brush
8 Driver's seat, cut away
9 Toolbox with all major track, engine, and general tools cleaning kit, fuel funnel, rolls of tape, etc.
10 Foot controls: clutch, foot-brake and accelerator, from left to right
11 Flame gun fuel and propellant hoses
12 Flame gunner/co-driver's seat
13 Auxiliary charging set
14 Sten SMG
15 Machete in sheath, above water-bottle
16 Ten 20-round Thompson, or eight 32-round Sten magazines
17 Stowage for Bren tools, portable cooker, spare track pins spare jettison lead, anti-gas suit, etc.
18 Crocodile flame gun
19 Hand brake

Plate G1: *Trooper, 107 Regiment RAC, 34 Tank Brigade; Battle of the Reichswald, February 1945*
The trooper, evidently from the crew of an SHQ Close Support tank, holds a round of 95mm High Explosive Mark 1A. He wears the black Royal Armoured Corps beret with the cap badge of his parent regiment; 107 RAC was formed from the King's Own Royal Regiment (Lancaster), and wore a gold lion above the legend *The King's Own*, all pinned through a red cloth patch. The 1943 tank suit was waterproof, warmly lined with khaki shirting material, and well endowed with zips and stud-fastened pockets.

Plate G2: *L/Cpl., 'C' Sqn, 7th Royal Tank Regiment; Han River, Korea, winter 1950-51*
The uniform consists of the 1949 open-collar battledress and the black RTR beret with silver cap badge. The shoulder-straps of the BD blouse bear the red and green tally of 7 RTR,. The white tank arm badge of the RTR is worn on the upper

'C' Squadron, 7 RTR fording the Imjin River. The leading vehicle, Gerald, shows the squadron's tactical number and brigade sign with the shipping serial below. Following regimental tradition, the tanks' names began with the letter 'G'

and were painted in block capitals on the lower part of the air louvres; other names known to have been used in Korea include George, Glynis and Gynaeolator (!) See front cover. (Major B. H. S. Clarke, RTR)

right arm, between the black and white 'frozen orifice' patch of 25th Infantry Brigade Group, and the rank chevron. He holds a round of 75mm Supercharge High Explosive ammunition.

Arranged around these two figures, to constant scale, are further examples of ammunition used by the Churchill:

a: 6pdr. High Explosive Mark 10T. Almost invariably fired from tanks with a tracer in the projectile base.

b: 6pdr. APC (Armour Piercing with Cap). A solid shot fitted with impact cap, and a tracer in the base of the projectile.

c: 6pdr. APC, BC (Armour Piercing with Cap, Ballistic Cap). Similar to the APC round but fitted with a thin-gauge streamlined ballistic cap.

d: 6pdr. APDS (Armour Piercing, Discarding Sabot). Introduced in mid-1944, this round utilized the principle of an accelerating tungsten carbide core within a disintegrating sabot, to achieve penetration at super-velocity.

e: 95mm Howitzer, Base Emission Smoke. Thi contained four smoke canisters activated by a bursting charge below the fuse ring. Useful fo target indication, or for 'blinding' the defence.

f: 95mm Howitzer, HEAT (High Explosiv Anti-Tank). A shaped-charge round which gav the Close Support tanks an anti-tank capability and which could also be used for bursting ope ferro-concrete fortifications.

INDEX

(References to illustrations are shown in **bold**. Plates are shown with page and caption locators in brackets.)